Dot Painting

12 SKILL-BUILDING PROJECTS TO MASTER TOOLS & TECHNIQUES

LEISURE ARTS, INC. • Maumelle, Arkansas

Introduction

Why try dot painting?

The real question here is, why not? It's literally love at first dot! And you probably already have everything you need to give it a go. Dot painting is a calming, relaxing, and meditative way to express yourself, creatively. "Dotting" is art therapy at it's finest and will help clear your mind of all other thoughts. You heard me right, ALL other thoughts...POOF...gone! As you lay your dots, one by one, the only thing that really comes to mind at all is, "Hmm..I wonder which color should I use next?" It's seriously just that wonderful! Dot painting can aide in reducing stress, anxiety, depression, and in one students discovery, it can even lower your heart rate! In other words, it's a great way to wind down the day.

People with self proclaimed, "very little creativity" or "too little patience", are also falling in love with dotting and finding it to be much easier than they thought and incredibly fun to do, as well as pretty cheap to try, and super rewarding. Speaking of rewarding, some have even turned their artworks into extra income. People from around the globe are discovering with their finished piece that they ARE creative after all! It's similar to paint by number or diamond painting but with so much more freedom and you, too, CAN do it! I'll give fair warning though, dot painting is VERY ADDICTING! Lay a few dots, and just like that, a new creative obsession is born. Once you dot, you can't stop! With everything becoming a target for the thought of, "I'd dot that!" But don't take my word for it.

(Tag me in your social media project posts and use #iddotthat so I can see your creations!)

One final but IMPORTANT note to consider before you start – mistakes happen and THAT'S OKAY! Clean it up and move on. No biggie! No one else will even notice! Most of the time we are our own worst critics. Sometimes you have to put the painting down, step away and take 5. When you come back to it, before you start, prop it up and look at how beautiful it is from across the room. Also, don't discard or paint over those first few attempts, you're going to absolutely love to see how far you've grown in a few days, weeks, and months from now! Keep in mind, we are not machines, we're human and we all make mistakes. If someone wants a flawless design, let them enjoy something computer generated. Don't expect perfection, doing so only sets us up for disappointment which could otherwise be completely avoided. There is no right or wrong in art. Don't compare your work to others, we're all individuals with our own strengths, weaknesses, and tastes. You WILL get better and better the more projects you create and the more dots you lay. Be easy on yourself. And most importantly, ENJOY THE PROCESS.

Inspiration

Color and design inspiration is literally EVERYWHERE! Sunsets, sunrises, plants and animals, clothing and tapestries, even furniture. Paint swatches & color wheels are also great for reference, too.

Meet Lydia May

Lydia May is a dot mandala artist & teacher born and raised in Cincinnati, Ohio. She has been teaching dot art on her YouTube channel where she gives step by step instruction on how to paint dot mandalas. Between homeschooling her three young children, the occasional date night with her boyfriend, taking her puppy Pablo for walks, and operating her own artist supply shop; the Dot Art Depot, she enjoys being in nature which is her favorite muse. Since starting her dot art journey in 2017, she has made countless friends from all over the world, from her Facebook mandala sharing group, and Instagram. Lydia is beyond grateful for all the friends and partnerships that this experience has afforded her and to be truly living her dream. You can find Lydia's original artworks on her website, www.DotArtDepot.com.

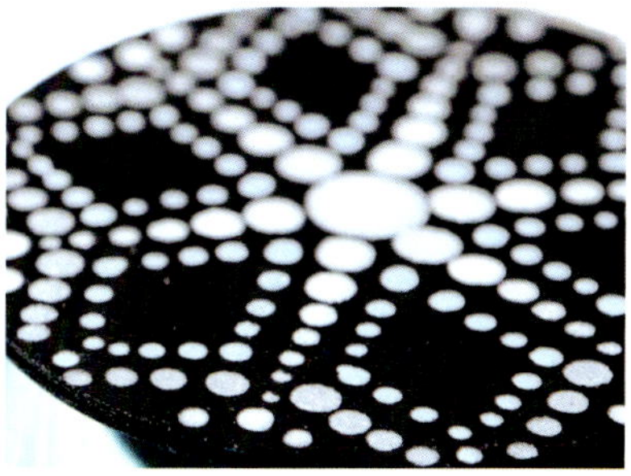

Contents

Tools

You can dot with all kinds of objects! Round and flat makes for clearly defined dots. Here are the tools I used in this book's projects.

Pencils and cotton swabs

A brand new pencil eraser offers a flat, round, surface for a uniform dot. Semi-sharpen the other end to create a dotting tool that will make your dots descend in size, just like a nail stylus would. To make cotton swabs into tools you will want the type that have paper sticks, the plastic kind doesn't work for this application. On one end of your cotton swab, remove all cotton and on the other end smear on a thin coat of paint, smoothing out the cotton while rubbing inward toward the stick. Allow to dry & you're ready to go!

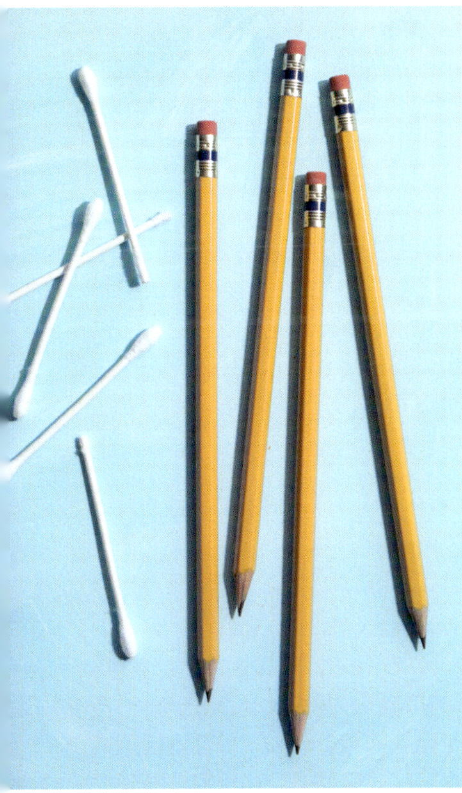

Crochet hooks

Crochet hooks that have a totally flat end on the handle will give you a perfectly round dot. Susan Bates® Crystalites® Crochet Hooks are great! There are two sets to chose from (or get them both!). The larger 4 piece set (8mm - 11.5 mm), and smaller 5 piece set (4mm - 6.5mm) are colorful and easy to hold and use. There is also an all white Susan Bates hook set that has 6 pieces (3.75mm - 6.5mm), comparable to the Crystalites 5 piece set, but with one extra size. You can reference the size of the tool at the end of each handle. To clean and maintain your hooks, just gently wipe them clean with a lightly dampened cloth in between each color and after each use.

Wooden dowels

Wooden dowels come in many sizes. You can purchase a pack of dowels that will have a variety of sizes from most craft stores for only a few bucks. Dowels are quite inexpensive and perfect to get you on the road to dotting! For my color-coded 16-piece dowel set, visit my online store, the Dot Art Depot, at www.dotartdepot.com. To clean and maintain your dowels, just gently wipe them clean with a lightly dampened cloth in between each color and after each use.

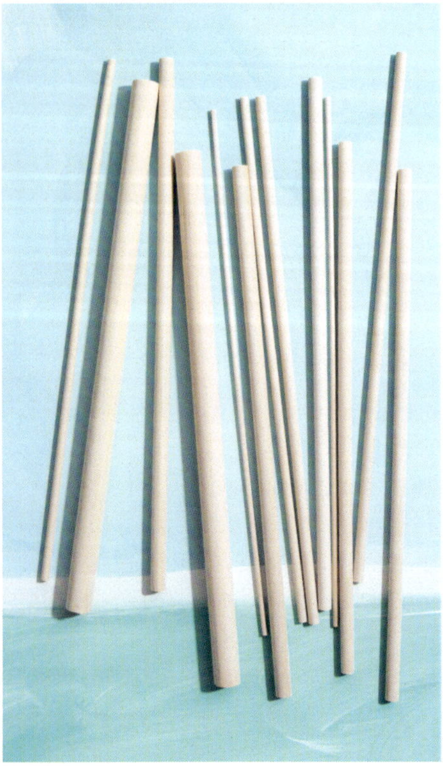

Painted Wooden Dowel Reference Table

Size	Color	Size	Color
3/32"	Black	23/64"	Gold
1/8"	White	3/8"	Sky Blue
5/32"	Blue	7/16"	Lime
3/16"	Pink	1/2"	Yellow
7/32"	Silver	5/8"	Orange
1/4"	Lavender	3/4"	Red
19/64"	Green	7/8"	Mint
5/16"	Purple	1"	Gray

Nail Stylus Dotting Tools

Last, but not least, (and maybe the best part!) for the tiny dots, nail stylus or embossing tools will do the trick! They are little round metal balls on a stem, with a handle, that you dip in paint and simply dot continuously, using the same amount of pressure, and the dots will descend in size like magic! They are perfect for adding lots of intricate detail to your paintings. I reference mine as 5 being the largest and 1 being the smallest. To clean and maintain your tools, just gently wipe them clean with a lightly dampened cloth in between each color and after each use.

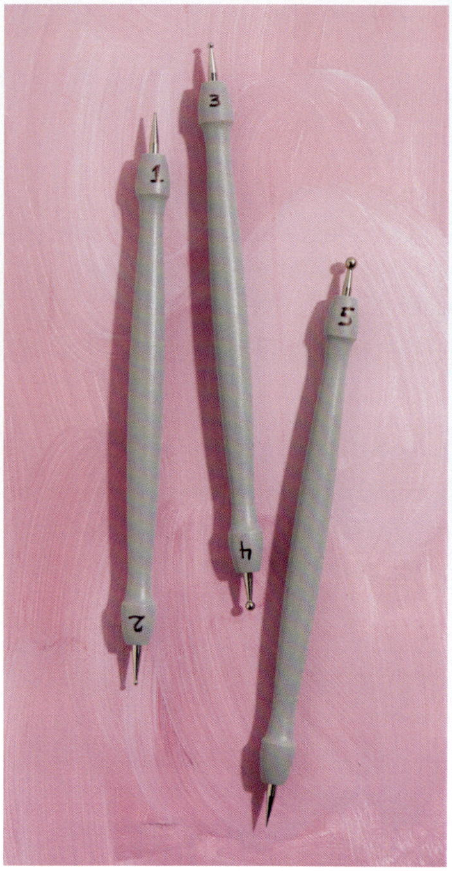

The above listed items are what I used for the projects in this book, however, this is not all that works for dots! Keep in mind you're looking for totally flat ends and no beveled edge. A lip balm cap end, an old cork, a flat nail head, a marker end, a toothpick, a skewer, a sewing pin head, a sewing needle end, a bobby pin, and even a paint brush handle end are all possibilities. The brush end of a small round paintbrush works wonderfully too but may take a bit more practice to master. All of these things are options. And it doesn't stop there! The list can go on. Literally all kinds of things can be used. Be creative and use what you have. The main goal is to HAVE FUN with it!

Dotting Tools Comparison Chart

A word about the tools used in this book – I am demonstrating various tools alongside each project, however, you can use them interchangeably following this handy dandy reference guide.

Wood Dowel	Crochet Hook	Cotton Swab	Pencil	Nail Stylus
			Sharp Tip	Size 5
1/8"	4mm			
3/16"	5mm	Prepped Tip		
	5.5mm			
1/4"	6mm		Eraser	
	6.5mm			
5/16"	8mm			
	9mm			
3/8"	10mm			
7/16"	11.5mm			
1/2"				
5/8"				

Paints

Acrylic craft paint works perfectly for dot painting. Acrylic is a water-based paint that has a fast drying time. Bottles of acrylic craft paint are easy to use with no fuss and are relatively inexpensive. Plus one bottle lasts SO LONG, since you literally only use one drop at a time. Enamel and Multi-surface acrylic paints are a bit thicker and will dry with a glossy finish, while regular acrylic paint is thinner and will dry with a matte finish. Every person has their own opinion on which look they like better and some even interchange within the two types. (I do sometimes!) While you can find acrylic paint in tubes, most tube paints tend to be quite thick and require more mixing and experimenting with to get the right texture for dotting. Ultimately, you're looking for a paint consistency similar to sour cream.

Here are some paint brands I have found to be perfect for dotting, right from the bottle with no fuss!

- DecoArt®
- Plaid® Folk Art®
- Craft Smart®
- Martha Stewart®
- Anita's®
- Apple Barrel®
- and lots more!

A tip for removing the plastic seal on paint bottles is to twist clockwise while pulling up and it will come right off! Acrylic paint settles and can separate into layers so don't forget to shake your paints well before use. I find that if I'm not mixing colors or tints, I'll just use a small amount of paint right from the paint cap to dip my tool in. If I am going to mix however, I will grab a paint palette. You can find reusable plastic paint palettes for around a dollar. Once you use it, you can wash it out or let the paint dry and peel it out, most of the time, very easily. (and kinda fun!)

Also, I have seen some friends line their palettes with plastic wrap or aluminum foil, for even easier cleanup. A disposable plate will also work in a pinch as a substitute palette. I like to add a drop of paint to lids with no color sticker and allow it to dry for a quick and easy true color reference, because some paints dry darker.

I like to use black or darker paint colors as a basecoat often because it really makes the other colors POP! But you can use any color of paint that you desire. Different colors play off of each other in different ways so play around and experiment to find neat color combos that you enjoy using!

Substrate

Dot painting can be done on almost any surface! Rocks are a great place to start and can be free right from your driveway! Card stock, canvas board, stretched canvas, glass & ceramics, wooden pendants, circles, or boxes, plastic chargers, metal plates, and even shoes and clothing!! You name it, it can be dotted! Most people like to start with rocks. There are a number of places to find rocks. Home improvement stores sell bags of beach stones in their garden centers. Landscape supply companies have an array of stones of all shapes, color, and sizes to choose from, as well. They are usually priced with very reasonable rates of cents per pound. When looking for rocks to paint, keep in mind, smoothness is key. If you cannot find smooth rocks, you can fill in small craters with a compound and once dry, sand it smooth to your liking.

Environmental tip- Please do not take from parks or rivers without first finding out your local laws on rock removal.

Clean your stones. Soap & water should be enough to remove any dirt. It's important to make sure your rock is free of residue or the paint won't adhere correctly. Let your rocks dry in the sun, or for immediate use, dry it off with a cloth. Your rock will need to be completely dry to start. I find doing this step in bulk is a great way to go because when you're ready to paint, you can just grab one and get started.

Stencils

For my stencils, visit my online store, the Dot Art Depot, at www.dotartdepot.com. Before creating my stencils I used a 360° protractor and a ruler. To use these, simply follow the project instructions to determine the number of slices to divide the design into. Divide 360 by the number of slices. So, for example, if the project says 4 slices. Divide 360 by 4, which equals 90. Place the protractor on the substrate and use a slate chalk marker to mark at 90°, 180°, 270°, and 360°. At that point, use a ruler to continue the guidelines across the substrate and you're ready to go.

Sealer

For lasting protection, you will want to seal your paint. There are also lots of ways to coat and seal your projects. Varnish and lacquer come in both spray and brush on types and will offer either a glossy finish or a matte finish. Matte = dull and not shiny, while gloss or semi gloss will keep a shine once dry. Both are a personal preference in the overall look of your completed project. I personally find spray on varnishes to be the easiest and quickest method. There is also a coating called epoxy resin that is thick and glossy and can have absolutely beautiful results and also adds extreme durability. Just make sure you are in a well ventilated area when using any varnishing product and follow all safety precautions & procedures on product labels.

Pro tip- Protect your table before starting by lining it with newspaper or a cheap poster board. And have cotton swabs nearby for quick and easy clean ups!

Other Useful Supplies

- paint palette
- ruler
- compass
- 360° protractor
- slate chalk marker
- dry erase marker
- large flat paint brush
- kneaded eraser
- flow and gel mediums

Peppermint Spiral

WHAT YOU'LL NEED

- ☐ approximately 3" to 3½" diameter stone
- ☐ Apple Barrel® Matte acrylic paint – Black
- ☐ DecoArt® Americana® Gloss Enamels™ multi-surface acrylic paints – True Red and White (or any colors you love!)
- ☐ wooden dowels – white (⅛"), pink (3⁄16"), lavender (¼"), purple (5⁄16"), sky blue (⅜"), lime (7⁄16"), and yellow (½")
- ☐ wide flat paintbrush
- ☐ guideline stencil (optional, from www.dotartdepot.com)
- ☐ damp rag and cotton swabs for cleanup
- ☐ sealer of your choice

PREP

1. Clean the rock and let dry completely.

2. Apply Black paint to basecoat the top of the rock or whole rock **(Fig. 1)**. Let the paint dry completely.

Fig. 1

LET'S GET STARTED!

Note: *Using a damp cloth, clean your tools after using each paint color.*

1. Using the purple tool, dip the tip in red paint and place the first dot in the center of the stone. If you have a stencil guide, you can use it to help you find the projects center. Switch to the white tool and make the next four dots in a crisscross pattern as close to the center dot as you can but without touching the dots together. Make a dot to the top, bottom, left and right around the center dot **(Fig. 2)**. Keep in mind, you will be able to get closer as you get more dotting practice under your belt, so for now, give yourself plenty of room.

Fig. 2

Fig. 3

Fig. 4

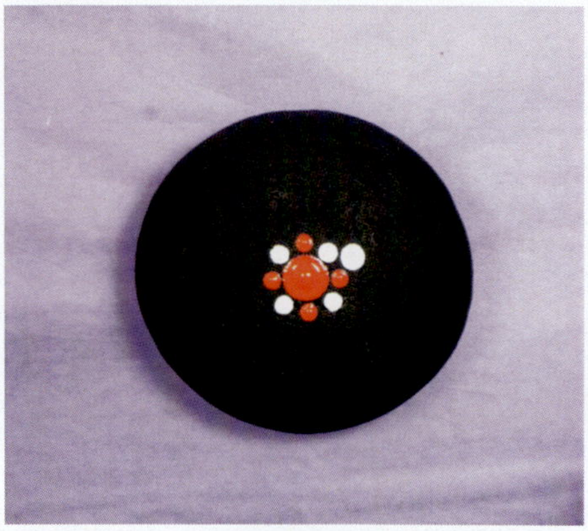

Fig. 5

2. With the same white tool in hand, switch to the white paint. This time, you will alternate the colors and fill in the space in between each dot with one white dot for a total number of 8 dots around the center **(Fig. 3)**.

3. Using the pink dowel, put a dot of white paint right in between **(Fig. 4)**, on the outer edge of the last two dots. You can go either way here, to the right or the left of the last white dot, but whichever way you choose, you will now need to stick to placing subsequent dots of the same color to that side in order to get the spiral effect by the end of the project. In my example, I chose to go to the right **(Fig. 5)**. Repeat this step for all four of the white dots **(Fig. 6)**.

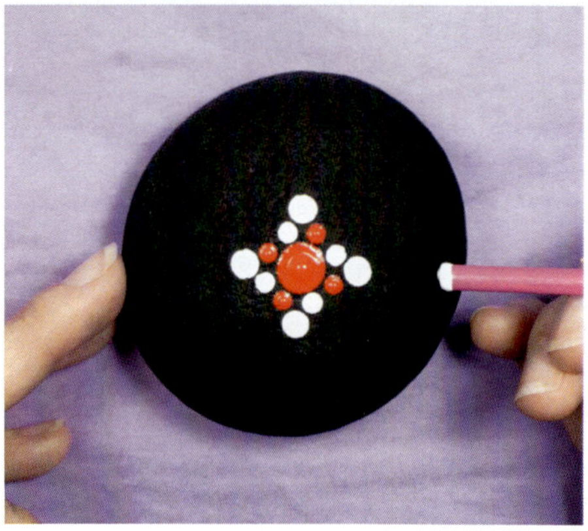

Fig. 6

4. With the same pink tool, dip the tool in red paint and dot in between each white dot of this row **(Fig. 7)**. The colors are alternating.

Fig. 7

Fig. 8

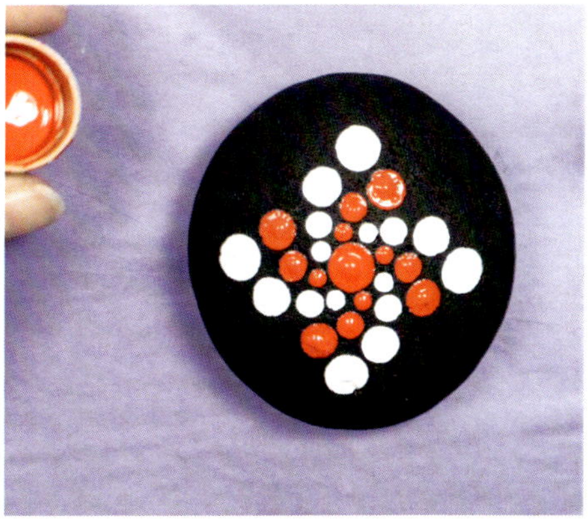

Fig. 9

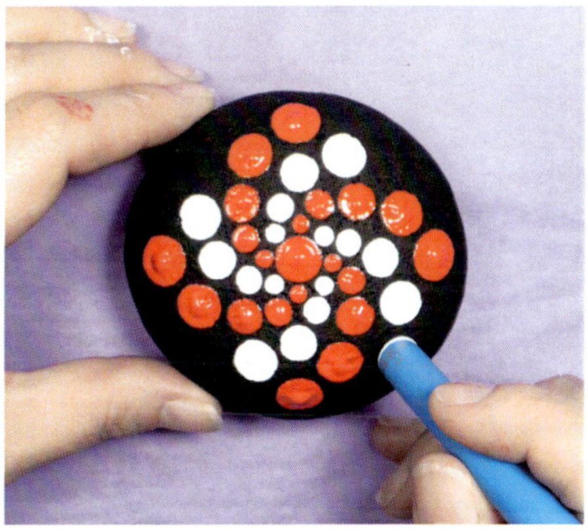

Fig. 10

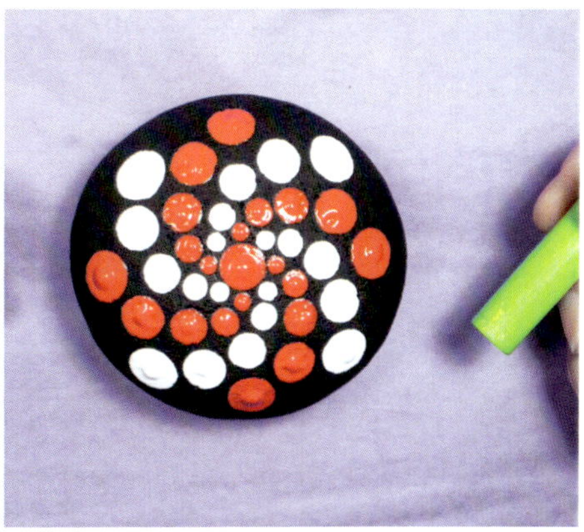

Fig. 11

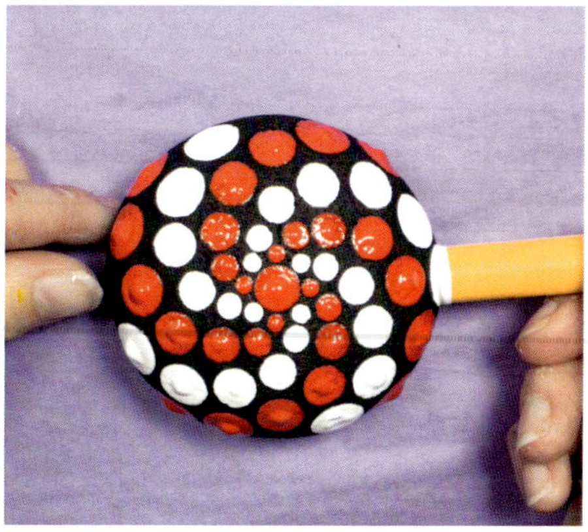

Fig. 12

5. Repeat these Steps, alternating colors, using in order of these tools; lavender, then purple, followed by sky blue, and then comes lime, and last use yellow **(Figs. 8-12)**.

6. Allow the paint to fully dry, giving it a minimum of a few hours. Overnight is ideal drying time before applying sealer to prevent smearing. Drying time will vary depending on elevation and weather.

Congratulations on your job well done on your first of many more dot art projects!

On to the next!

Rainbow Heart Stone

WHAT YOU'LL NEED

- ☐ approximately 4" to 5" stone
- ☐ Apple Barrel® matte acrylic paint - Black
- ☐ DecoArt® Americana® acrylic paints - Red Alert, Bright Orange, Golden Yellow, Festive Green, Peacock Teal, Bright Blue, Lavender, and Snow (Titanium) White
- ☐ DecoArt® Dazzling Metallics® - Splendid Gold
- ☐ flat 1" wide paintbrush
- ☐ prepared cotton swabs
- ☐ a new, mostly sharpened pencil
- ☐ damp rag and extra cotton swabs for cleanup
- ☐ sealer of your choice

PREP

1. Clean the rock and let dry completely.

2. Apply Black paint to basecoat the top of the rock or whole rock **(Fig. 1)**. Let the paint dry completely.

3. Apply a coat of sealer **(Fig. 2)**.

4. Trace the heart pattern onto paper; cut out. Use pattern to trace the heart with pencil on the bottom half of stone **(Fig. 3)**.

Fig. 1

Fig. 2

Fig. 3

necessities™ | nécessités | necesidades

LET'S GET STARTED!

Note: *Using a damp cloth, clean your tools after using each paint color.*

1. Using the cotton end of the swab tool, place a dot of Red Alert paint right on the guideline on either side of the heart, at about the midway point of the heart's curves, reloading the tool before each dot by dipping it in paint again **(Fig. 4)**.

Fig. 4

2. Following the traced design as your reference, use the paper stick end of the swab to place 2 dots above and 2 dots below the first dot, re-dipping the tool into paint with each dot as you go. Repeat on both sides **(Fig. 5)**.

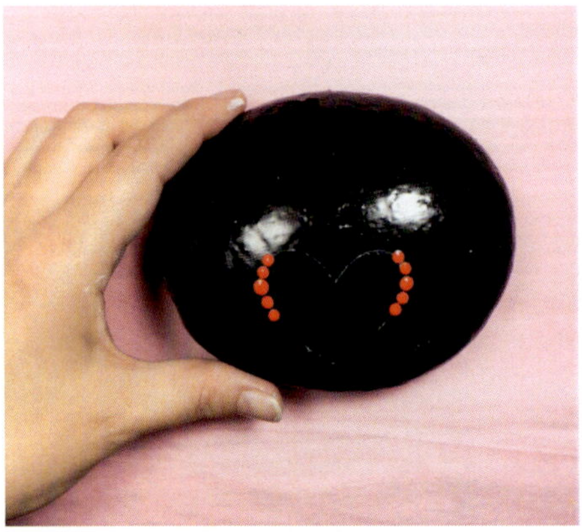

Fig. 5

3. Using the sharpened end of the pencil, dip it into the Red Alert paint once and follow the rest of the guideline, dotting all the way down to the bottom point of the heart. The dots will descend in size without changing the pressure in which you push and give a tapered look to the dots moving towards the heart's pointed end **(Fig. 6)**. Repeat on the top **(Fig. 7)**. Repeat on the other side **(Fig. 8)**.

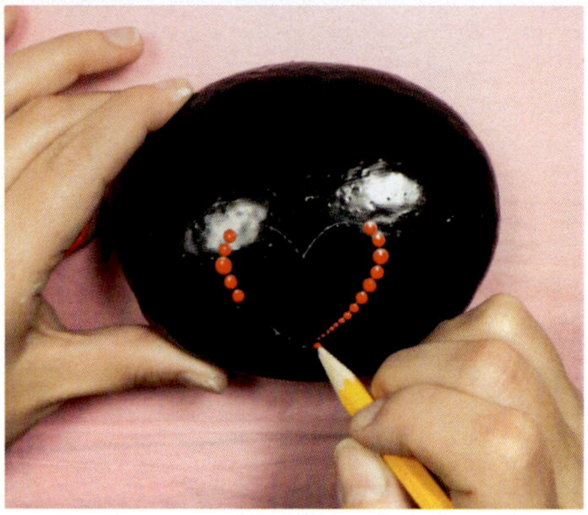

Fig. 6

Fig. 7

Fig. 8

4. Repeat Steps 1 - 3, moving inward in rows to fill in the heart with Red Alert dots, starting with the cotton end tool, followed by the stick end for 2 dots and then the pencil end for the tapering of the dots the rest of the way around the heart **(Fig. 9)**. I used my pencil end to paint a small heart in the very middle where there was a gap.

Fig. 9

5. Following a typical rainbow color scheme (red, orange, yellow, green, blue, indigo, and violet), the next color will be Bright Orange. Place the largest Bright Orange dot slightly above and right **(Fig. 10)**. Follow the same rules as the first row of Red Alert that you made except this time, don't dot all the way down to the bottom of the heart's

Fig. 10

Place your stunning creation in a plant or zen garden to enjoy!

point (**Fig. 11**). You do want the Bright Orange dots to meet at the top center.

Fig. 11

Fig. 12

6. Follow Step 5, swapping out the Bright Orange with the remaining colors in this order – Golden Yellow, Festive Green, Peacock Teal, Bright Blue, Lavender, Splendid Gold, and lastly, Snow (Titanium) White (**Fig. 12**).

7. Allow all paint to dry completely.

8. Apply a final coat of sealer to your design.

Simple Snowflake Magnet

WHAT YOU'LL NEED

- ☐ 2½" wood circle disk blank
- ☐ DecoArt® Americana® Gloss Enamels™ multi-surface acrylic paint – Black
- ☐ DecoArt® Extreme Sheen® Metallic paints – Sterling Silver, Sky Blue Topaz, & Silver
- ☐ prepared cotton swabs
- ☐ a brand new, mostly sharpened pencil
- ☐ damp rag and extra cotton swabs for cleanups
- ☐ wide flat paintbrush
- ☐ guideline stencil (from www.dotartdepot.com) or ruler
- ☐ slate chalk marker
- ☐ sealer of your choice for protection
- ☐ ¾" diamter self-adhesive craft magnetic dot

Fig. 1

Fig. 2a

PREP

1. Paint the wood disk with black paint and let dry completely (**Fig. 1**).

2. Trace out the guidelines using either a stencil or ruler (**Figs. 2a & 2b**). You want 6 equal slices.

Fig. 2b

LET'S GET STARTED!

Note: *Using a damp cloth, clean your tools after using each paint color.*

1. Using the eraser end of the pencil, place a dot of Sterling Sliver paint right on the center of the wood disk (**Figs. 3a & 3b**).

Fig. 3a

Fig. 3b

2. Using the stick end of the cotton swab tool and same paint color, place one dot on each of the six guidelines around the center dot (**Figs. 4a & 4b**). You want them to be as close as possible but without touching the center dot. However, do give yourself room here when first starting to practice dot painting. And if they do happen to run together, no biggie! Just use an unused cotton swab and clean it up by twirling the paint right up and away from the disk. You can always touch up the disk with more basecoat color as well, if needed. And then move on.

Fig. 4a

Fig. 4b

Fig. 5a

Fig. 6a

Fig. 5b

Fig. 6b

3. Using the sharpened end of the pencil, dip it into the same paint color. Start dotting on the guideline, next to the last dot, and dot continuously outward, staying on the guideline and stopping close to the outer edge of the disk (**Fig. 5a**). I counted 5 to 6 dots. Now you have six spokes to your snowflake, just like a real snowflake would have (**Fig. 5b**).

4. Moving on to the Sky Blue Topaz paint, start by dipping the pencil tip into the paint and placing the first dot right between the two larger dots in the "V." Make dots parallel to a spoke, moving outward towards the edge of the disk, for a count of 5 dots (**Fig. 6a**). Re-dip the pencil tip in paint, re-dot the first initial blue dot, and dot down the other side, parallel with the opposite spoke (**Fig. 6b**). Repeat on both sides of all six spokes (**Fig. 6c**).

Fig. 6c

5. Now, make a diamond shape by re-dipping the pencil into paint and this time dot from the last dot of blue and make a straight line towards the center edge in between the spokes. Repeat to the other side moving towards the center, making a diamond shape out of blue dots (**Fig. 7a**). Repeat on all six spokes (**Fig. 7b**).

Add a personalized message on the back and give this one as a gift or a perfect stocking stuffer. Or keep it to hang your favorite picture on your fridge.

Fig. 7a

Fig. 7b

Fig. 8a

Fig. 8b

6. Use the pencil tip once more, but this time with the Silver paint. Make a row of dots parallel to the bottom two edges of the blue diamond dots **(Fig. 8a)**. Repeat on all six diamonds **(Fig. 8b)**.

7. Finally, using the Sterling Silver paint, make 3 dots under the Silver dots at the end of each spoke **(Fig. 9)**. And you have made a cute little snowflake!

8. Once the paint is fully dry, seal it for a shiny finish. Place a magnetic dot in the center of the back **(Fig. 10)**.

Congratulations on another job well done!

On to the next!

Fig. 9

Fig. 10

Coral Jewelry Dish

WHAT YOU'LL NEED

- ☐ 4½" diameter terra cotta clay saucer
- ☐ DecoArt® Americana® acrylic paints – Royal Navy
- ☐ DecoArt® Americana® Multi-Surface Satin™ acrylic paints – Vanilla Shake and Coastal Waters
- ☐ DecoArt® Americana® Gloss Enamels™ multi-surface acrylic paint – Coral Blush
- ☐ DecoArt® Dazzling Metallics® acrylic paint – Splendid Gold
- ☐ Susan Bates® crochet hooks - sizes 4mm, 6mm and 8mm
- ☐ nail stylus dotting tools
- ☐ wide flat paintbrush
- ☐ damp rag and extra cotton swabs for cleanups
- ☐ sealer of your choice

PREP

1. Using Royal Navy, paint the saucer and allow it to dry completely **(Fig. 1)**.

2. Apply sealer for a shiny appearance **(Fig. 2)**.

LET'S GET STARTED!

Note: *Using a damp cloth, clean your tools after using each paint color.*

1. Locate the center of the saucer. Mine was easy and had a slight indent right where the center is. With the Vanilla Shake paint and 8mm crochet hook, make the center dot **(Fig. 3)**.

Fig. 1

Fig. 2

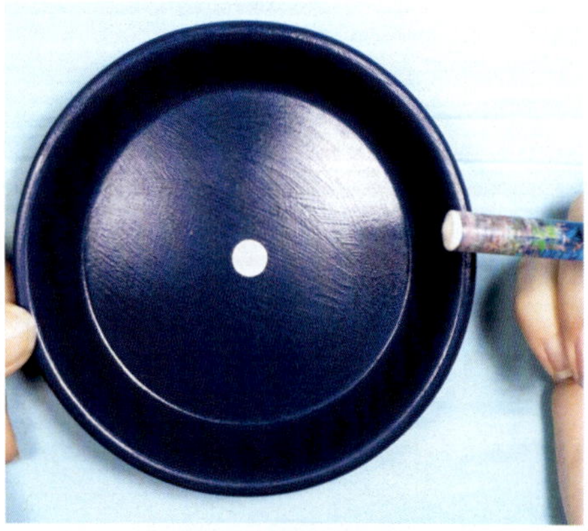

Fig. 3

2. With Coral paint, create a ring of small dots around the center dot. Use the size 2 nail stylus and make a crisscross of dots to the top, bottom, left, and right, close to the center dot but without touching it (**Fig. 4a**). Once you have four dots, add another dot in between each of those to get eight dots (**Fig. 4b**), and then add another dot right in between each of those to get a total of sixteen dots around the center dot (**Fig. 4c**).

Fig. 4a

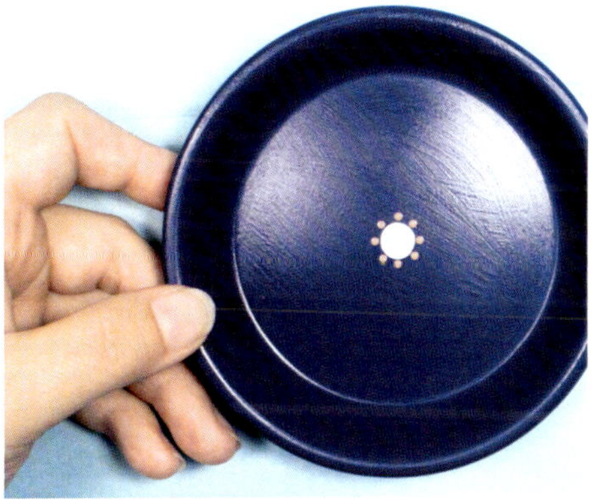

Fig. 4b

Fig. 4c

3. The second ring of dots will be offset from the first row and just a little bit larger. Using Coastal Waters paint and the size 5 nail stylus, place a dot on the outer edge, in between two dots of the previous row. Continue placing dots to fill in each of the sixteen spaces around the first ring to have two complete rings (**Figs. 5a - 5c**).

Fig. 5a

Fig. 5b

Fig. 5c

4. Using the size 4mm crochet hook and Splendid Gold metallic paint, place a dot offset from the last row on the top, bottom, left, and right (**Fig. 6a**) and then one more in between those for a total of 8 Splendid Gold dots (**Fig. 6b**).

Fig. 6a

Fig. 6b

5. Now, make the Splendid Gold dots into petals by wrapping little "bridges" of Vanilla Shake paint around each one. Using the size 1 nail stylus, dip in paint and start with the first dot lining up in the center of the outer edge of the Splendid Gold dot and dot continuously down to the base of one side, hugging the curve of the Splendid Gold dot. Then re-dip the stylus in paint, re-dot that first initial dot and dot down to the base of the other side (**Fig. 7a**). Repeat around each of the eight Splendid Gold dots (**Fig. 7b**).

Fig. 7a

Fig. 7b

6. For the next step, use the 6mm crochet hook and place a dot of Coral paint slightly but not all the way down in between each of the Vanilla Shake bridges for a total of eight Coral dots (**Fig. 8**).

Fig. 8

7. Use the size 1 nail stylus and the Splendid Gold metallic paint to make three "tails" of dots right under the Coral dots, dotting toward the center (**Fig. 9**).

Fig. 9

8. Keep using the Splendid Gold metallic paint, but use the size 5 nail stylus and make little Splendid Gold bridges around the Coral dots (**Fig. 10**).

Fig. 10

9. Using Coastal Waters paint, place a dot in between the Splendid Gold bridges of the previous row using the 6mm crochet hook (**Fig. 11**).

Fig. 11

10. Use the size 4 nail stylus to make little Vanilla Shake bridges around the Coastal Waters dots (**Fig. 12**).

Fig. 12

11. Place a larger dot of Splendid Gold in between each of the Vanilla Shake bridges using the 8mm crochet hook (**Fig. 13**).

Fig. 13

12. Make a bridge of dots around the Splendid Gold dots using the size 4 stylus and Coral paint (**Fig. 14**).

Fig. 14

13. Make another bridge of dots around the bridges of Coral dots using the size 4 nail stylus and Coastal Waters paint (**Fig. 15**).

14. Place the last dot of Vanilla Shake in between the Coastal Waters bridges using the 6mm tool (**Fig. 16**).

15. Allow project to dry fully and coat with lacquer.

Fig. 15

Fig. 16

Enjoy your new jewelry dish for yourself or give it as a gift!

Peacock Stone

WHAT YOU'LL NEED

- ☐ approximately 4" stone
- ☐ Apple Barrel® Matte acrylic paint – Black
- ☐ DecoArt® Extreme Sheen™ Metallic Acrylic Paint - Bronze and Peridot
- ☐ FolkArt® Metallic Color Shift™ - Aqua Flash
- ☐ Craft Smart® Multi-Surface Premium Ultra Bright Metallic Acrylic paint - Sapphire
- ☐ wooden dowels – white (⅛"), pink (3⁄16"), lavender (¼"), purple (5⁄16"), sky blue (⅜"), and lime (7⁄16")
- ☐ nail stylus dotting tools
- ☐ wide flat paintbrush
- ☐ damp rag and cotton swabs for cleanups
- ☐ sealer of your choice

PREP

1. Clean the rock and let dry completely.

2. Apply Black paint to basecoat top of the rock or whole rock **(Fig. 1)**. Let paint dry completely.

Fig. 1

LET'S GET STARTED!

Note: *Using a damp cloth, clean your tools after using each paint color.*

1. The first dot on this stone will all be done with Peridot paint. To start, using the lime dowel, make one dot in the center of the stone **(Fig. 2)**.

Fig. 2

2. With the size 5 nail stylus, make a crisscross of dots around the center dot, one to the top, bottom, left, & right. Then place a dot in between each of those dots to get 8 dots around the center. And then place one more dot in between each of those dots to make a total of 16 dots around the center dot **(Fig. 3)**.

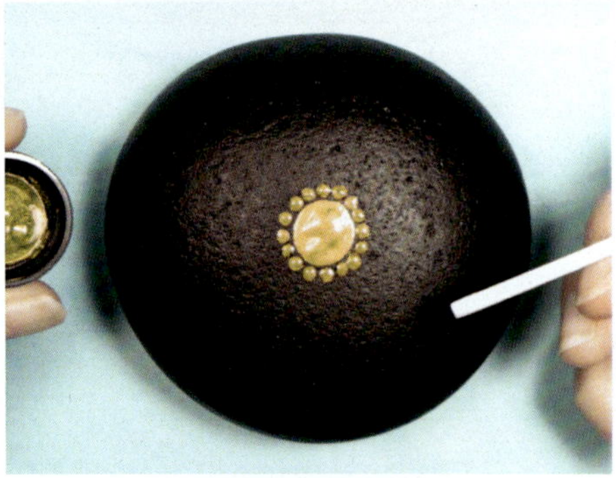

Fig. 3

3. Switch to the white dowel and place a dot in between, on the outer edge, of two dots on the previous row of dots. Make a dot in between each set of dots all the way around to make a full second row of dots **(Fig. 4)**. These dots are off set from the first row of dots.

Fig. 4

4. Repeat Step 3, creating four more rings of dots, each off set from the previous ring using this order of tools - pink dowel for ring three **(Fig. 5)**, lavender dowel for ring four **(Fig. 6)**, purple dowel for ring five **(Fig. 7)**, and lastly the sky blue dowel for the last ring **(Fig. 8)**.

Fig. 5

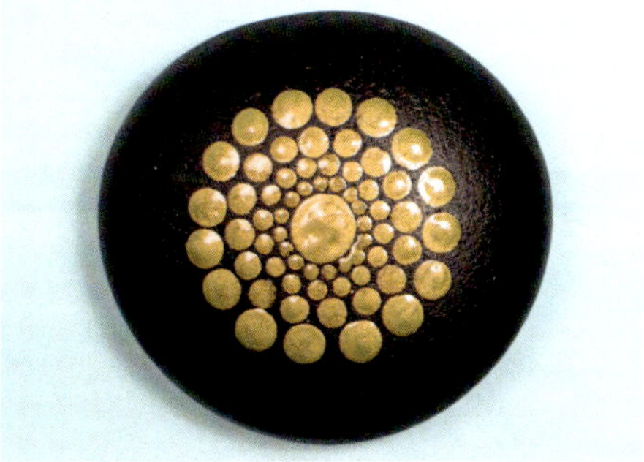

Fig. 6

Fig. 7

Fig. 8

5. Let all of these dots dry completely before moving to the next steps.

6. This is where you add dots on top of dots. I call them "top dots." Use Bronze paint and the purple dowel to make the first dot right in the middle of the center dot **(Fig. 9)**. Basically what you're doing is making each top dot a bit smaller than the dot under it, leaving just a ring of the previous color exposed. This will be the rule for the rest of the painting.

Fig. 9

7. For the first ring of top dots, use the size 4 nail stylus. This time, the dots aren't centered. You're going to line them up to the edge that is closest to the center dot, so that just like the peacock feather looks, the dots too will have the effect of little half moons of color on top of color **(Fig. 10)**.

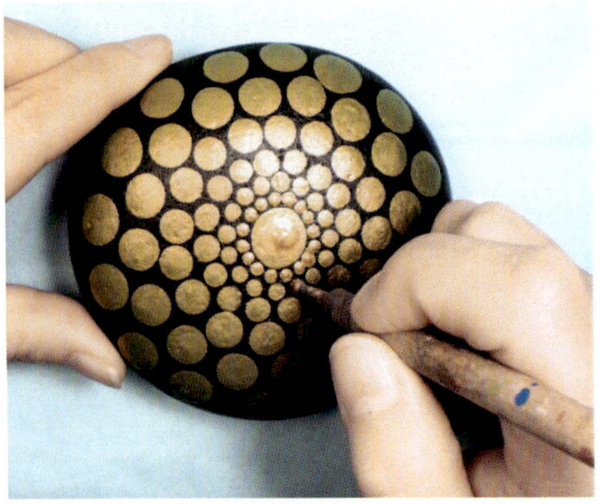

Fig. 10

8. Repeat Step 7 for the next subsequent rows in this order, size 5 nail stylus for the second ring **(Fig. 11)**, white dowel for the third ring **(Fig. 12)**, lavender dowel for the fourth ring **(Fig. 13)**, and the purple dowel for both the fifth and sixth rings **(Fig. 14)**.

Fig. 11

Fig. 12

Fig. 13

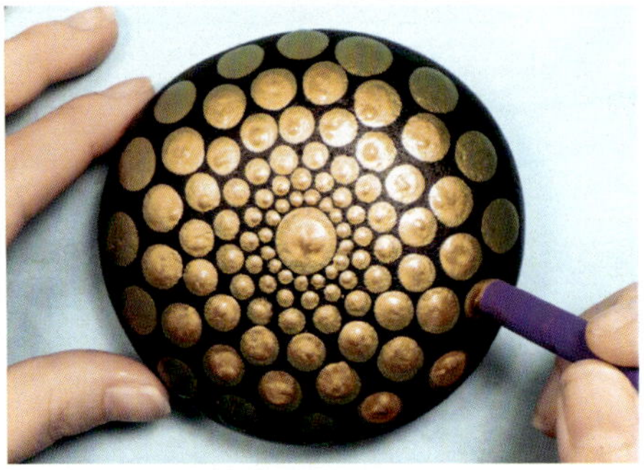

Fig. 14

9. Allow second row of paint to fully dry before moving on.

10. For the third top dot you will use the Aqua Flash and make them smaller than the last row. Use the lavender dowel for the third top dot on the main center dot **(Fig. 15)**.

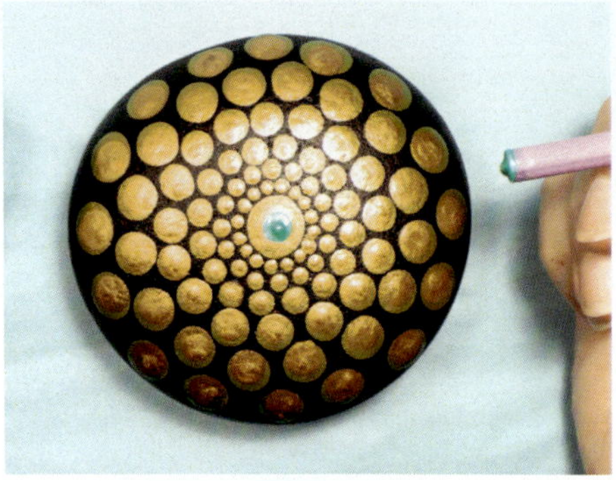

Fig. 15

11. The size 2 nail stylus will just fit for the tiny dots on the first ring **(Fig. 16)**. Remember to keep making them all point in toward the center dot; so hug that inner edge. If these, or any of the previous Steps are hard for you to see, skip it altogether! It's no big deal and I promise, it'll still look fantastic!

Fig. 16

Fig. 17

Fig. 19

Fig. 21

Fig. 18

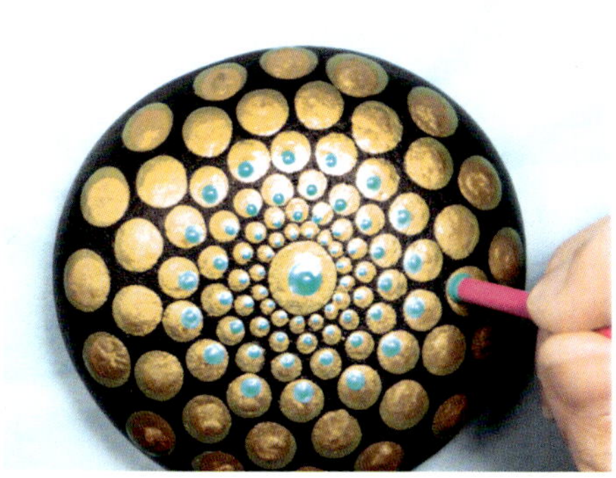

Fig. 20

12. For the second ring, use the size 3 nail stylus (**Fig. 17**). For the third ring use the size 5 nail stylus (**Fig. 18**). For the fourth ring, use the white dowel (**Fig. 19**). For the fifth ring, use the pink dowel (**Fig. 20**). And for the sixth ring use the lavender dowel (**Fig. 21**).

Fig. 22

Fig. 23

13. Make sure all layers are dry before moving on. Alright, for the fourth and final layer of top dots, use the Sapphire acrylic paint. Starting with the center dot, use the white dowel for the very center top dot (**Fig. 22**).

14. I completely skip the first row because it would require a needle to put another dot on that row. So moving on to the second row, use the size 1 nail stylus (**Fig. 23**).

15. Use the size 2 nail stylus for the third row (**Fig. 24**). Use the size 4 nail stylus for the fourth row (**Fig. 25**). And for the last row, use the white dowel (**Fig. 26**).

16. Let the final layer of paint dry fully, giving it overnight or even a couple of days before adding the sealer.

Fig. 24

Fig. 25

Enjoy your gorgeous creation!

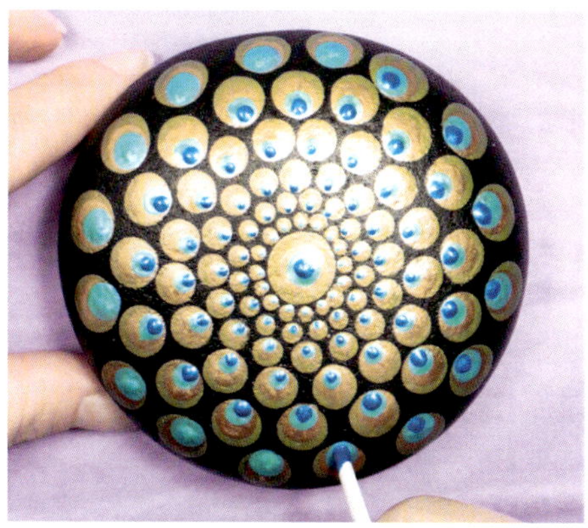

Fig. 26

Tropical Pendant

WHAT YOU'LL NEED

- ☐ 2¼" diameter wood circle disk
- ☐ Apple Barrel® Matte acrylic paint – Black
- ☐ Apple Barrel® multi-surface acrylic paint - Paradise Pink, Candy Apple, Outrageous Orange, and White
- ☐ FolkArt® Color Shift acrylic paints - Pink Flash, Red Flash, and Orange Flash
- ☐ Susan Bates® crochet hooks - sizes 4mm and 6.5mm
- ☐ nail stylus dotting tools
- ☐ guideline stencil or ruler (from www.dotartdepot.com)
- ☐ 1" wide flat paintbrush
- ☐ kneaded eraser
- ☐ drill with 1⁄16" to 5⁄64" drill bit
- ☐ 10mm jump ring
- ☐ chain
- ☐ damp rag and cotton swabs for cleanups
- ☐ sealer of your choice

PREP

1. Paint the wood disk by applying Black acrylic paint using the brush and turning the disk at the same time **(Fig. 1)**. If you want, you can go all the way out to the edge but I left a small ring unpainted **(Fig. 2)**. Allow the paint to dry completely.

Fig. 1

Fig. 2

2. Locate and mark the center **(Fig. 3)** and place a dot of Candy Apple paint with the 6.5mm crochet hook **(Fig. 4)**. Once that dot is completely dry, use a stencil or ruler and draw guidelines to make 8 equal slices **(Fig. 5)**. (Guidelines are completely optional but many find them very helpful to keep the design symmetrical.)

Fig. 3

Fig. 4

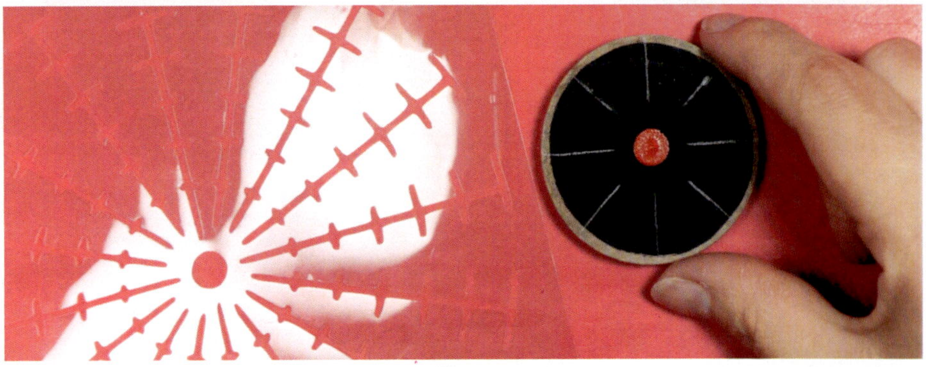

Fig. 5

LET'S DOT!

Note: *Using a damp cloth, clean your tools after using each paint color.*

1. With the Outrageous Orange paint, create a ring of small dots around the center dot. Use the size 2 nail stylus and make a crisscross of dots to the top, bottom, left, and right, close to the center dot but without touching it **(Fig. 6)**. Add another 2 dots in between each of those to get a total of 12 dots around the center dot **(Fig. 7)**.

Fig. 6

Fig. 7

2. The second ring of dots will be offset from the first ring and just a little bit larger. Using the Paradise Pink paint and the size 5 nail stylus, place a dot on the outer edge in between two dots of the previous ring (**Fig. 8**). Continue placing dots to fill in each of the spaces around the first ring to have a complete ring of 12 dots (**Fig. 9**).

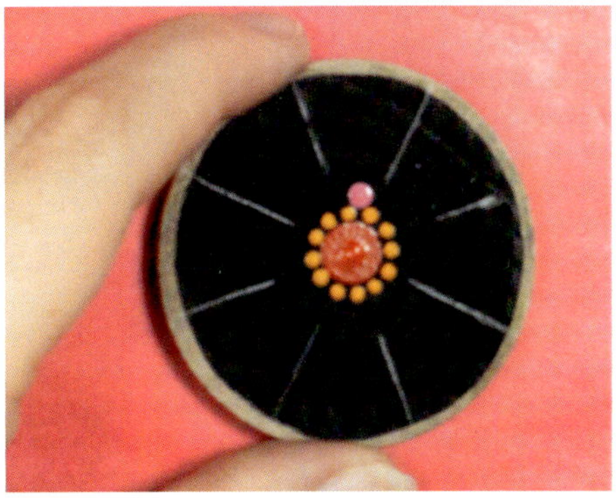

Fig. 8

Fig. 9

3. Repeat Step 2 using White paint and the 4mm crochet hook (**Fig. 10**).

Fig. 10

Fig. 11

Fig. 12

4. On each of the guidelines, place one dot of Candy Apple paint using the 6.5mm crochet hook for a total of 8 dots (**Fig. 11**).

5. Now make the Candy Apple dots into "petals" by wrapping little "bridges" of Paradise Pink paint around each one. Use the size 2 nail stylus, dip in paint and start off with the first dot lining up in the center of the outer edge of the Candy Apple dot and dot continuously down to the base of one side, hugging the curve of the Candy Apple dot (**Fig. 12**). Then, re-dip the stylus in paint, re-dot the first initial dot and dot down to the base of the other side (**Fig. 13**). Repeat around each of the eight Candy Apple dots (**Fig. 14**).

Fig. 13

Fig. 14

6. Using Outrageous Orange paint and the 4mm crochet hook, place one dot in between, on the upper edges of each of the larger Candy Apple dots (**Fig. 15**). Try and leave a little bit of room to make tiny bridges around them.

Fig. 15

7. Using the Outrageous Orange paint and size 2 nail stylus, place a tail of dots in between each of the larger Candy Apple dots tapering in towards the center dot **(Fig. 16)**.

Fig. 16

8. Using the size 1 nail stylus and White paint, make little bridges around the Outrageous Orange dots **(Fig. 17)**.

Fig. 17

9. Allow the project to fully dry.

10. Now it's "top dot" time! Start off with the size 4mm crochet hook and place a dot of the Red Flash paint in the center of each of the Candy Apple dots **(Fig. 18)**.

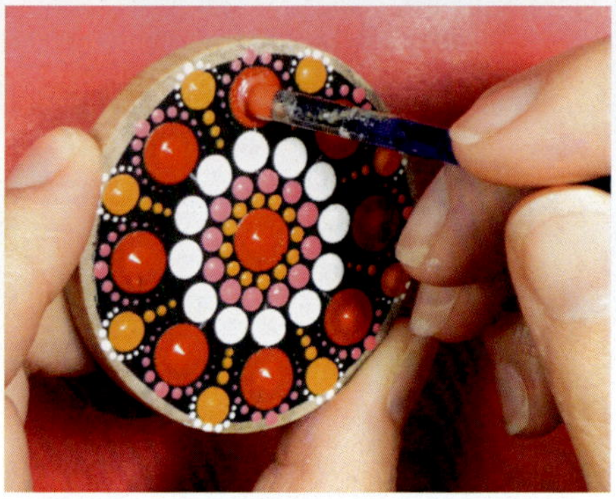

Fig. 18

11. Next, use Pink Flash paint and the size 5 stylus to place a dot in the center of each of the White dots of the third ring **(Fig. 19)**.

Fig. 19

12. And lastly, use the Orange Flash paint and same size 5 nail stylus to place a dot in the center of each of the 8 outer Outrageous Orange dots **(Fig. 20)**.

Fig. 20

13. Allow it to fully dry again and remove all guidelines **(Fig. 21)**. I love to use a kneaded eraser for removing mine. They work wonders!

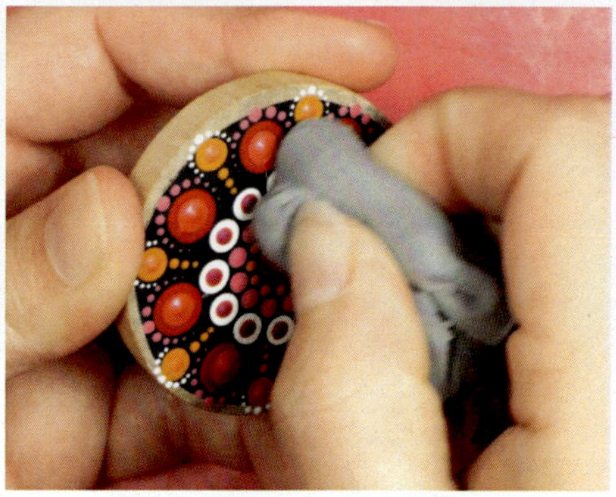

Fig. 21

14. Finally, add the sealer.

15. Once the top dots are fully dried, drill a hole in the edge of one side, add a jump ring and a chain **(Fig. 22)** and you're ready to wear your beautiful work of art

Fig. 22

Featuring the colors of the tropics, this pendant will remind you of your favorite trip to the islands.

Jade Rings

WHAT YOU'LL NEED

- ☐ 7" diameter wood circle
- ☐ Apple Barrel® Matte acrylic paint - Black
- ☐ DecoArt® Americana® Multi-Surface Satin™ - Turf Green
- ☐ DecoArt® Americana® Gloss Enamels™ multi-surface acrylic paint - Calypso Blue and White
- ☐ Craft Smart® Multi-Surface Premium Satin acrylic paint - Mediterranean and Teal
- ☐ Martha Stewart Crafts® Multi-Surface satin acrylic paint - Mermaid Teal
- ☐ Apple Barrel® Multi-Surface acrylic paint - Clover Fields
- ☐ gloss fluid medium
- ☐ wooden dowels - white (1/8"), pink (3/16"), lavender (1/4"), purple (5/16"), lime (7/16"), orange (5/8") and mint (7/8")
- ☐ nail stylus dotting tools
- ☐ guideline stencil (from www.dotartdepot.com) or 360° protractor
- ☐ compass
- ☐ slate chalk marker
- ☐ wide, flat paint brush
- ☐ damp rag and cotton swabs for cleanups
- ☐ sealer of your choice

PREP

1. Apply black acrylic basecoat to the wood circle **(Fig. 1)** and let paint dry completely.

Fig. 1

2. As needed, thin out the thicker paints with a few drops of fluid medium **(Fig. 2)**. This helps the dots not have a hard peak as most multi-surface and enamel paints will have if left alone to dot with. If you like the hard peaks, leave it as it is and move forward.

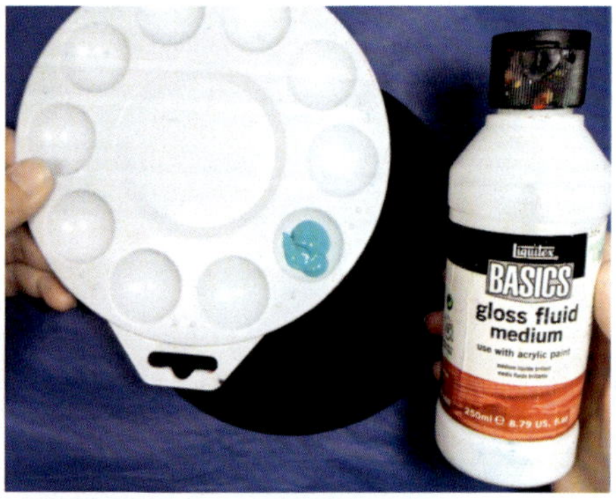

Fig. 2

LET'S GET STARTED!

***Note:** Using a damp cloth, clean your tools after using each paint color.*

1. We are starting off center so you have freedom here. Mark a "center" 2" away from the side. This is where you will reference all other markings from. Starting with the Mint dowel and the Mediterranean paint, make a center dot **(Fig. 3)**. Allow this dot to fully dry before adding guidelines.

Fig. 3

2. Make guidelines around the center dot to make sure all guidelines are lined up correctly **(Fig. 4)**. It can be difficult at times to get the center dot right in the center of the drawn

Fig. 4

guidelines if done the other way around. Use the compass to draw concentric circles from the center of the dried center dot in increments of 1" out, 1¼" out, 2" out, 3" out, 3¾" out, and 4¼" out. Yours do not have to follow mine, they just really help keep all the dots in nice, straight rings. Add the guidelines using either a guideline stencil (**Fig. 5**) or protractor, and make 16 slices around the center dot.

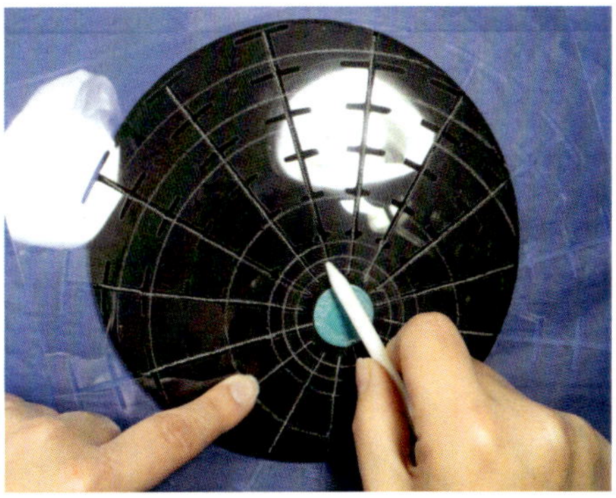

Fig. 5

3. With the white dowel and Clover Fields paint, make a crisscross of dots around the center dot, one to the top, bottom, left, & right. Then place a dot in between each of those dots to get 8 dots around the center. And then place one more dot in between each of those dots to make a total of 16 dots around the center dot (**Fig. 6**).

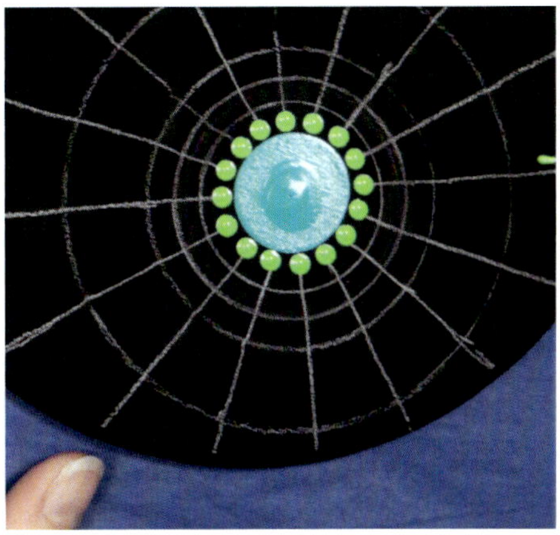

Fig. 6

4. At this point, if you have the room and are comfortable with making tiny dots, use the size 1 nail stylus and place two small Clover Fields dots to the top and the bottom in between each of the dots (**Fig. 7**). This is only to fill in space and can be skipped if you want. It's just a personal preference.

Fig. 7

5. Switch to the pink dowel and Teal paint and place a dot in between each of dots of the previous ring to make a full second ring of dots (**Fig. 8**). These dots are off set from the first ring of dots.

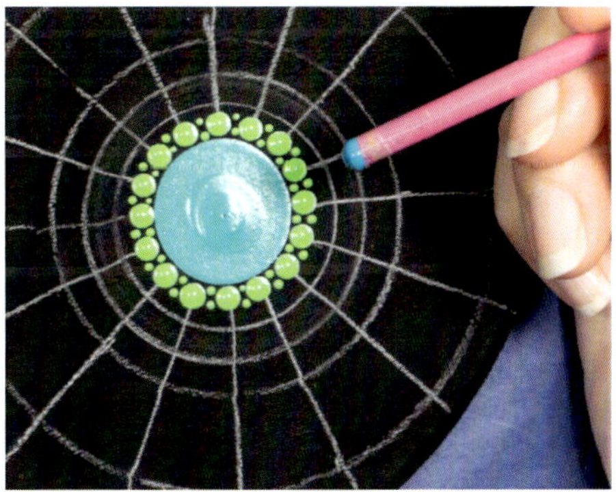

Fig. 8

6. Using the size 1 nail stylus and Teal paint, repeat Step 4 to add small dots.

7. Using the lavender dowel and Calypso Blue paint, repeat Step 3 to make a third ring (**Fig. 9**).

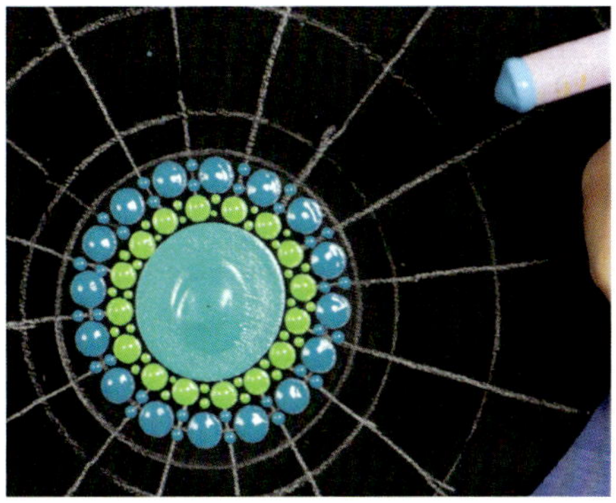

Fig. 9

8. Using the size 4 nail stylus dotting tool and White paint, repeat Step 4 to add small dots (**Fig. 10**).

Fig. 10

9. Repeat Step 5, but this time using the lime dowel with Mermaid Teal paint for this ring of dots (**Fig. 11**).

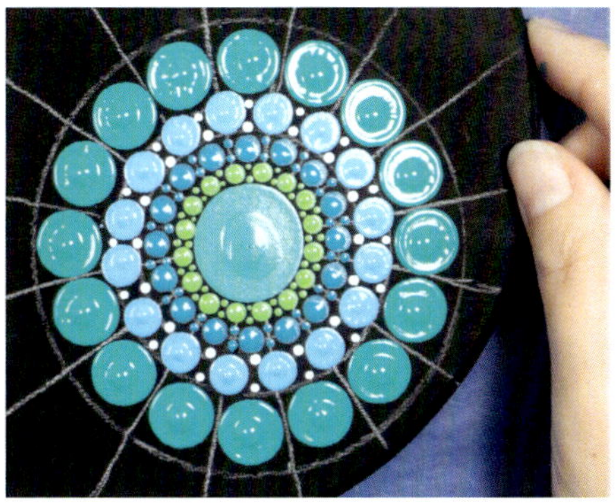

Fig. 11

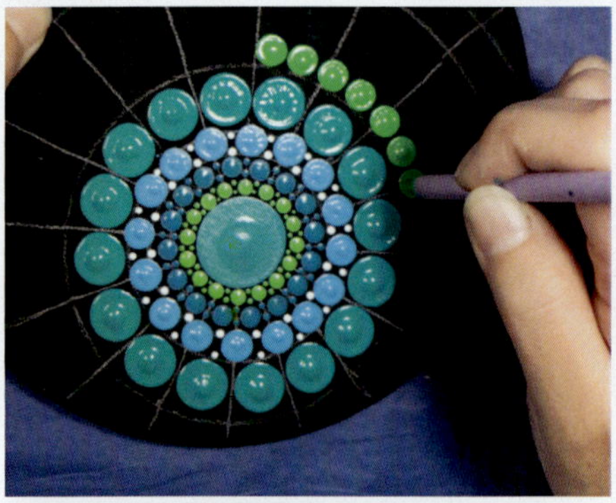

Fig. 12

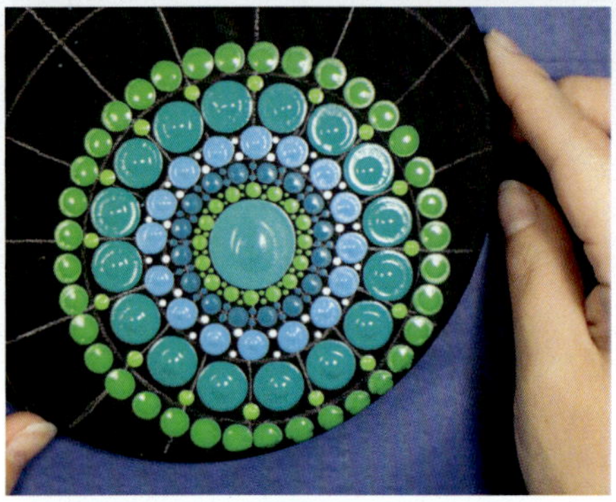

Fig. 13

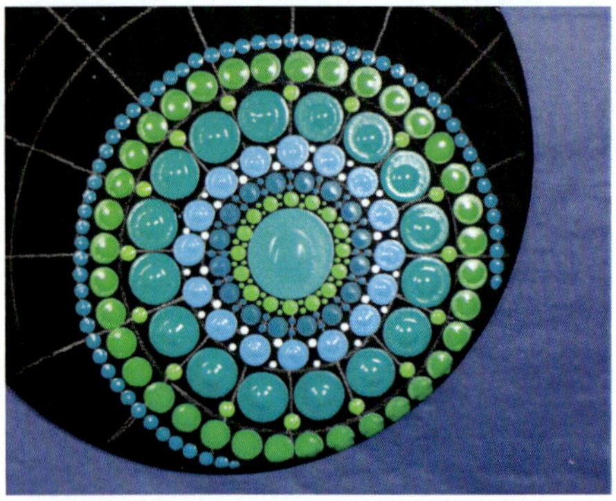

Fig. 14

Fig. 15

10. Going back to the lavender dowel, use the Turf Green paint and make a ring of dots around the guideline **(Fig. 12)**. One tip I have found that works best to keep a nice straight ring is if you stick to one side of the guideline instead of dotting right ON the guideline. Pick a side and try to keep the dots lined up to that side all the way around. In this step, I see that 2-2½ dots fit in each slice, but I wasn't counting and I found that just enough dots fit around the ring, just make sure they are side by side.

11. Add a small dot of Clover Fields dots in between each of the Mermaid Teal dots (between the Mermaid Teal ring and the Turf Green ring), using the white dowel **(Fig. 13)**.

12. Here I wanted to break up the design a bit and add some detail with a few smaller dot rings. Using the white dowel and the Teal paint, start the dots right next to and follow the guideline **(Fig. 14)**. This is my favorite part of this design because from here on out, the rings are going to fall off the circle, so it doesn't matter as to where you START dotting.

13. Right next to the teal ring, add a ring of Calypso Blue with the pink tool, again, starting wherever **(Fig. 15)**.

14. With the orange dowel and Clover Fields paint, make a ring of dots next to the previous ring, starting wherever **(Fig. 16)**.

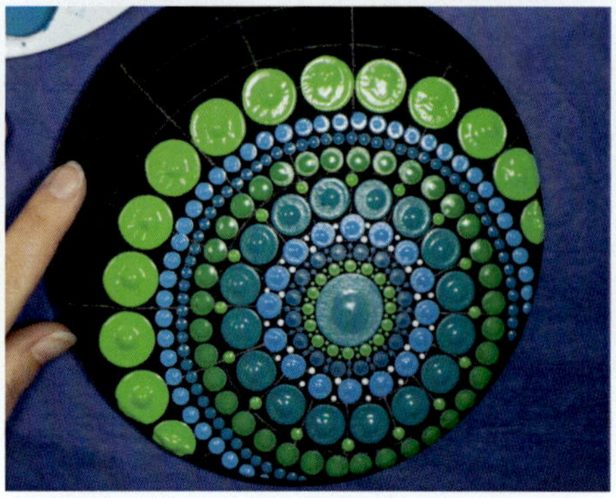

Fig. 16

15. With the size 4 nail stylus dotting tool and White paint, we're going to wrap little "bridges" of white paint around the outer edges of the larger green dots. Use the size 4 nail stylus dotting tool, dip in white paint and start with the first dot lining up in the center of the outer edge of the green dot and dot continuously down to the base of one side hugging the curve of the green dot **(Fig. 17)**. Then re-dip the stylus in paint, re-dot that first initial dot and dot on down to the base of the other side **(Fig. 18)**. Repeat around each of the green dots **(Fig. 19)**.

Fig. 17

Fig. 18

Fig. 19

Display your handiwork on an easel tucked away on a shelf.

16. If you, at any point, need more guidelines, you can use the compass to draw on more as long as it is beyond the wet paint **(Fig. 20)**. For the next step, use the purple dowel and place a dot of Mediterranean paint slightly, but not all the way, down between each of the white bridges **(Fig. 21)**.

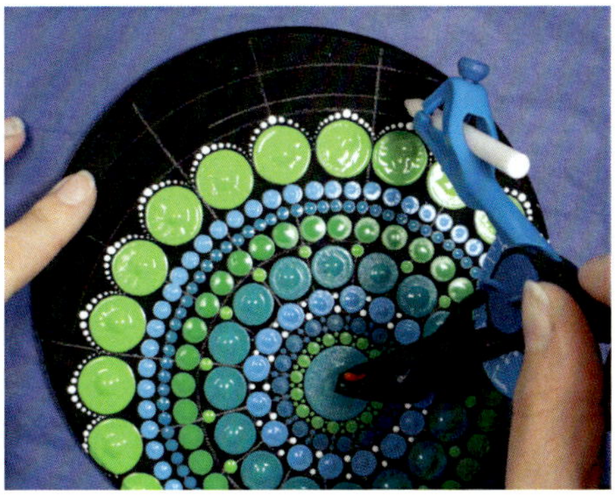

Fig. 20

Fig. 21

17. To either side of the Mediterranean dots, use the same color and make smaller dots with the white dowel **(Fig. 22)**.

Fig. 22

18. Almost finished! Make the next ring right along the guideline using the Mermaid Teal and lavender dowel. Add a small dot of Turf Green using the white dowel under and in between each of the large Clover Fields dots just to fill in space **(Fig. 23)**.

Fig. 23

19. And finally, for the last ring use Teal and the green dowel to finish off the piece **(Fig. 24)**. If you have more room, fill it out with another ring using some Turf Green or even a ring of white.

Fig. 24

Look at your progress! You have completed another amazing piece of dot art and you should be very proud! Apply a coat of spray lacquer to protect your piece.

On to the next!

Star Tile Coaster

WHAT YOU'LL NEED

***Note:** For durability, your paints should be permanent or self-sealing. Please read the product labels carefully as not all paints are permanent or self-sealing.*

- ☐ 4¼" square ceramic tile
- ☐ DecoArt® Americana® Gloss Enamels® paint - True Red, White, and Antique Gold
- ☐ DecoArt® Americana® Multi-Surface Satin™ paint - Coffee Bean
- ☐ wooden dowels – white (⅛"), pink (3⁄16"), and lavender (¼")
- ☐ nail stylus dotting tools
- ☐ dry erase marker (optional)
- ☐ ruler
- ☐ guideline stencil (from www.thedotartdepot.com) or 360° protractor
- ☐ damp rag and cotton swabs for cleanup
- ☐ rubbing alcohol
- ☐ paper towels
- ☐ sealer of your choice

PREP

1. Prepare the tile by cleaning it with rubbing alcohol and a paper towel to get it good and thoroughly clean.

2. Lining up the ruler from corner to corner, use the dry erase marker to draw two small lines to mark the center **(Fig. 1)**. (Guidelines are completely optional but many find them very helpful to keep the design symmetrical.) Using White paint and the purple dowel, apply the first dot to the middle of the tile **(Fig. 2)**. Allow the dot to completely dry. Rub away the dry erase marker from the center.

3. Use a guideline stencil **(Fig. 3)** or a 360° protractor and mark off six evenly spaced slices **(Fig. 4)**. I line mine up to where one set is in the center of two sides. This step is to get the dot spacing started off right.

Fig. 1

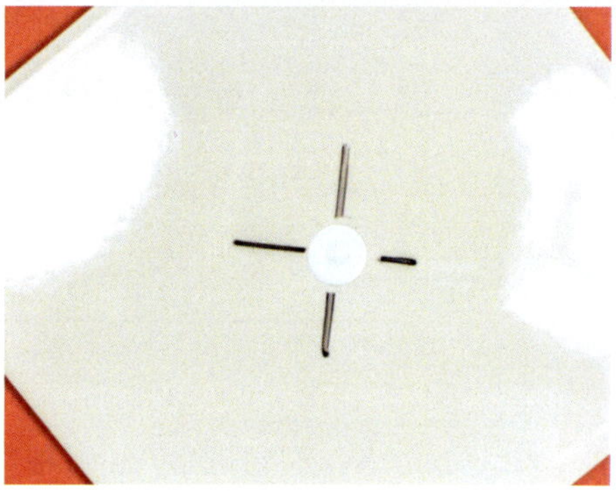

Fig. 2

Fig. 3

Fig. 4

LET'S DOT!

***Note:** Using a damp cloth, clean your tools after using each paint color.*

1. The first ring is going to be made with the size 5 nail stylus and White paint. Make a dot on each of the six guidelines **(Fig. 5)**. Then make one dot in between each of those to get a total of 12 dots around the center dot **(Fig. 6)**. Then rub away the guidelines **(Fig. 7)**.

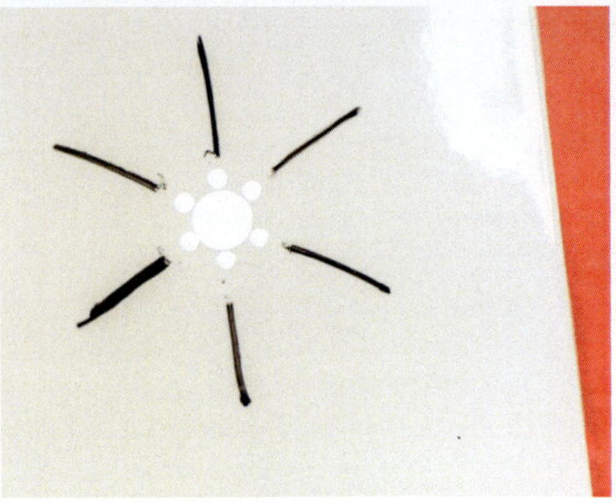

Fig. 5

Fig. 6

Fig. 7

2. The second ring will be made with White paint, too, but this time use the white dowel. Place a dot right in between, but on the outer edge of two dots from the previous ring, so that they are offset from each other **(Fig. 8)**. Place a dot in the spaces between each of the previous 12 dots for a full second ring around the center dot.

Fig. 8

3. Using the lavender dowel and True Red paint, make a dot as if you were going to start another ring, but this time only place dots in between every other set of dots **(Fig. 9)**. You will have a total of 6 True Red dots.

Fig. 9

4. To make a few different tints of True Red paint, pour a bit of White paint in two of the wells of the palette **(Fig. 10)**. In one well, add just a drop or two of True Red and in the other make it a 1:1 ratio of True Red and White paint **(Fig. 11)**. Mix them using a stylus (or whatever is lying around) to get two different tints of pink paint **(Fig. 12)**.

Fig. 10

Fig. 11

Fig. 12

5. Now we're going to make the True Red dots into "petals" by wrapping little "bridges" of the light pink paint around each one. Using the size 5 nail stylus, dip in paint and start with the first dot in the center of the outer edge of the True Red dot and dot continuously down to the base of one side, hugging the curve of the dot (**Fig. 13**). Then re-dip the stylus in paint and re-dot the first dot and dot down to the base of the other side (**Fig. 14**). Repeat around each of the six True Red dots (**Fig. 15**).

Fig. 13

Fig. 14

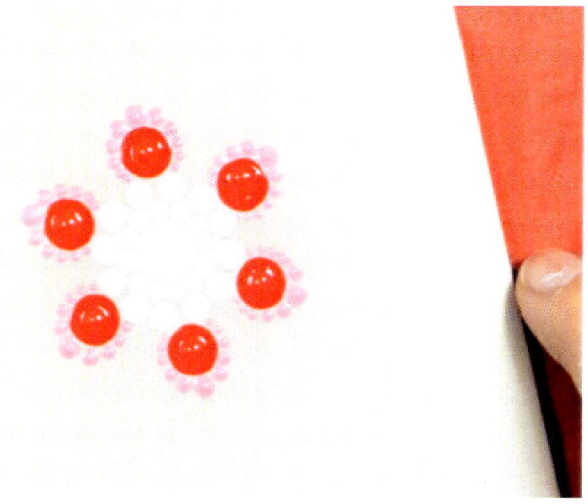

Fig. 15

6. Switching to the dark pink paint that you made, use the white dowel to make one dot right above the largest main dot of the previous bridge of light pink dots. Do this to all six "petals" (**Fig. 16**). This will be the main dot on the second bridge and will start to make the six petals larger.

Fig. 16

7. Now, using the size 5 nail stylus and the dark pink paint, make the first dot right next to the main dot and dot all the way down to the base, hugging the previous bridge of dots (**Fig. 17**). There is no particular number of dots to fit in there, just whatever works that you are comfortable with placing in that space. However, I find it helpful to count along. I was able to fit five down each side, so I counted, "one, two, three, four, five." Re-dip the stylus in paint and count down the other side. Now the petals are growing! Do this to each side of each petal.

Fig. 17

8. Repeat Step 6 using True Red paint and the pink dowel for the main dot to make the beginning of the third bridge of the first six petals of this design (**Fig. 18**).

Fig. 18

9. For the next dot down in this bridge, use the white dowel and place a smaller True Red dot on each side of the base of the main True Red dot (**Fig. 19**).

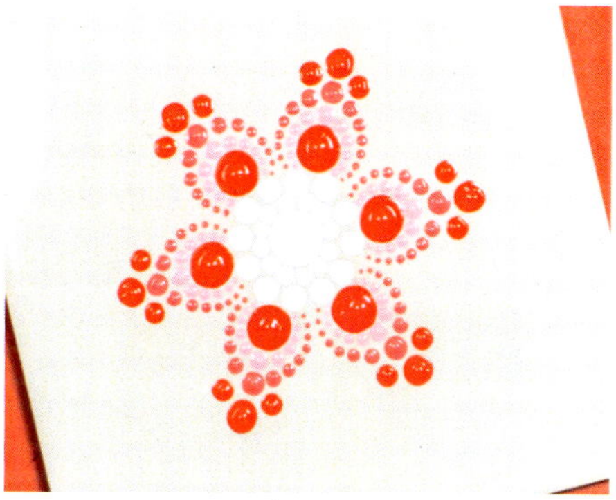

Fig. 19

10. Use the size 5 stylus and use True Red paint and dot continuously down to the base of the petal on one side, and then re-dip the stylus, and repeat on the other side **(Fig. 20)**. And that is the first set of petals.

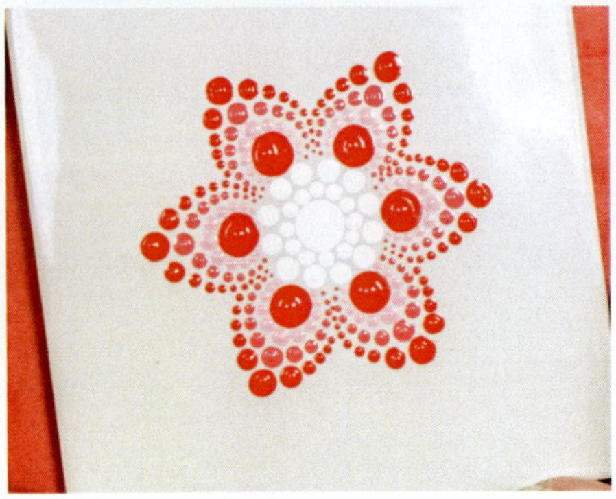

Fig. 20

11. To make a few different tints of Coffee Bean paint, pour a bit of White paint in two of the wells. In one well, add just a drop or two of Coffee Bean and in the other make it a 1:1 ratio of Coffee Bean and White paint **(Fig. 21)**. Mix them, using a stylus (or whatever is lying around), to get two different tints of brown paint.

Fig. 21

12. Using the lavender dowel and Coffee Bean paint, place the dots right between the True Red petals, offset from the first row of petals **(Fig. 22)**.

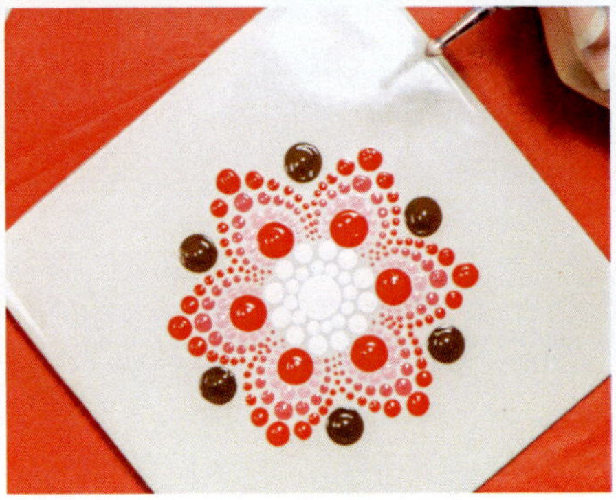

Fig. 22

13. Repeat Steps 5-10 to make 6 brown petals using light brown, dark brown, and Coffee Bean paints **(Figs. 23 - 25)**.

Fig. 23

Fig. 24

Fig. 25

14. Using the lavender dowel and White paint, make 6 white dots in between the brown petals **(Fig. 26)**.

Fig. 26

15. Repeat Step 5 and use Antique Gold paint to wrap a little "bridge" around each white dot **(Fig. 27)**.

Fig. 27

Use your creation as a coaster by using permanent paints.

16. Add a ring of "top dots" of Antique Gold paint to the first ring of white dots around the center dot using the size 2 nail stylus (**Fig. 28**).

Fig. 28

17. Add a ring of "top dots' of Antique Gold paint to the second ring of white dots around the center dot using the size 4 nail stylus (**Fig. 29**).

Fig. 29

18. Repeat Steps 6 - 10 and use Antique Gold paint to complete the gold petals (**Fig. 30 - 31**).

Fig. 30

Fig. 31

19. For the paint to become permanent, you should bake the tiles. You should always double check for the correct baking time and temperature for the brand of paint you're using. For the paints used in this book, allow the paint to cure for 4 days. Then place tile in a cool oven, set temperature to 325° F, and bake for 30 minutes. Allow the item to cool in the oven with the door partially open. Some other brands will self-seal by just waiting for 28 days instead of baking them.

Blissful Mini Canvas

WHAT YOU'LL NEED

- ☐ 5" square stretched mini canvas
- ☐ Apple Barrel® Multi-Surface satin acrylic paint - Princess Purple
- ☐ Apple Barrel® Outdoor Indoor Gloss acrylic paint - Turquoise and Purple Velvet
- ☐ FolkArt® Enamels™ paint - Cobalt Hue
- ☐ FolkArt® Multi-Surface Satin acrylic paint - Magenta
- ☐ DecoArt® Americana® Gloss Enamels™ multi-surface acrylic paint - White
- ☐ DecoArt® Americana® acrylic paint - Baby Blue
- ☐ DecoArt® Americana® Multi Surface Satin™ - Blue Bird
- ☐ damp rag and cotton swabs for cleanup
- ☐ Susan Bates® crochet hooks - 4mm, 5.5mm, 6mm, 8mm, and 11.5mm
- ☐ nail stylus dotting tools
- ☐ ruler or guideline stencil (from www.dotartdepot.com)
- ☐ slate chalk marker
- ☐ wide, flat paint brush
- ☐ sealer of your choice for protection

PREP

1. Paint the canvas in an ombré fade effect created using a wider brush. Paint ⅔ of the canvas with Baby Blue. Then, while that paint is still wet, add a small amount of darker Blue Bird paint to the bottom of the canvas **(Fig. 1)** and blend upward towards the center of the canvas without going back over the darker paint at the bottom or going over the lighter blue paint at the top **(Fig. 2)**. Allow the canvas to dry completely.

Fig. 1

Fig. 2

2. Use the ruler or stencil and draw on guidelines from corner to corner and from the center edge of one side of the canvas to the other side **(Fig. 3)** . Use ruler or guideline stencil to divide canvas into 16 equal slices **(Fig. 4)**.

Fig. 3

Fig. 4

LET'S DOT!

Note: *Using a damp cloth, clean the tools after using each paint color.*

1. Locate the center of the canvas and using the Purple Velvet paint and 8mm crochet hook, make the center dot **(Fig. 5)**.

Fig. 5

2. With Turquoise paint, create a ring of small dots around the center dot. Use the size 3 nail stylus and make a crisscross of dots to the top, bottom, left, and right, close to the center dot but without touching it. Once you have four dots, add another dot in between each of those to get eight dots, and then add another dot right in between each of those to get a total of sixteen dots around the center dot **(Fig. 6)**.

Fig. 6

3. The second ring of dots will be offset from the first ring and just a little bit larger. Using Cobalt Hue paint and the size 5 nail stylus, place a dot on the outer edge in between two dots of the previous ring (**Fig. 7**). Continue placing dots to fill in each of the sixteen spaces around the first ring to have two complete rings (**Fig. 8**).

Fig. 7

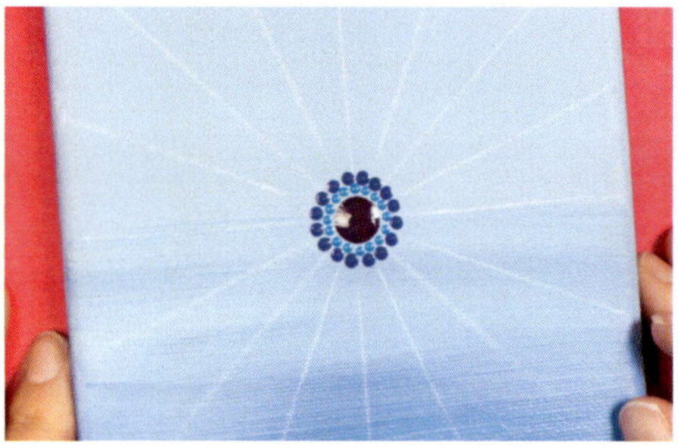

Fig. 8

4. Using the size 6mm crochet hook and Magenta paint, place a dot offset from the last ring on the top, bottom, left, and right and then one more in between those for a total of 8 Magenta dots (**Fig. 9**).

Fig. 9

5. Make the magenta dots into "petals" by wrapping little "bridges" of White paint around each one. Use the size 4 nail stylus, dip in paint and start off with the first dot lining up in the center of the outer edge of the magenta dot (**Fig. 10**) and dot continuously down to the base of one side hugging the curve of the magenta dot (**Fig. 11**). Then re-dip the stylus in paint, re-dot that first initial dot and dot on down to the base of the other side. Repeat around each of the eight magenta dots (**Fig. 12**).

Fig. 10

Fig. 11

Fig. 12

6. Use the 4mm crochet hook and place a dot of Princess Purple paint slightly but not all the way down in between each of the white bridges, for a total of eight dots (**Fig. 13**).

Fig. 13

7. Place dots of Purple Velvet starting above each of the little white "bridges" using a size 4 nail stylus and next to them a dot to either side with a size 3 stylus (**Fig. 14**).

Fig. 14

8. Use the 11.5mm crochet hook and make a large dot of Turquoise paint right above the 8 small Purple dots (**Fig. 15**).

Fig. 15

9. Place a white dot on the center edge right above each of the largest dots using the 5.5mm crochet hook (**Fig. 16**).

Fig. 16

10. Starting next to the white dot and using the size 5 nail stylus, make consecutive dots down to the base of one side hugging to the curve of the large dot (**Fig. 17**). Then re-dip the tool in white paint and dot the same way down the other side (**Fig. 18**). Repeat for all 8 dots (**Fig. 19**).

Fig. 17

Fig. 18

Fig. 19

11. In the next few Steps you'll be creating 3 "tails" in between the white bridges. Using the size 5 nail stylus and the Cobalt Hue paint, lay a "tail" of dots, starting in the middle, dotting towards the center of the canvas. Line up the first dot with the white bridge edge (**Fig. 20**). Repeat with 3 tails between each petal (**Fig. 21**).

Fig. 20

Fig. 21

12. The next dot on each tail will be a bit larger than the largest of the stylus dots and is going to be made right above it using a 4mm crochet hook **(Fig. 22)**.

Fig. 22

13. Now place one dot that is a bit larger than the previous dots only above the middle tail using a 5.5mm crochet hook **(Fig. 23)**.

Fig. 23

14. Now, create small tails made with Magenta paint using a size 5 stylus and dotting in between the larger tails **(Fig. 24)**.

Fig. 24

15. And for the last touch, once the first layer of dots is dry, add a "top dot" on top of the center dot using Princess Purple and the 5.5mm crochet hook **(Fig. 25)**. Add "top dots" of the Purple Velvet on top of the Princess Purple dots using the size 2 nail stylus **(Fig. 26)** to brighten up the middle.

This design lends itself well to other projects too. You could paint it on a beautiful keepsake box or impress friends and paint this design on a serving tray.

Fig. 25

Fig. 26

Listen, there are no rules in art so feel free to make changes to colors as you see fit. Also, playing around with top dot colors can be so much fun! Have fun with it!

This project is finished! Another amazing painting under the belt.

Way to go!

Love Mini Canvas

WHAT YOU'LL NEED

- ☐ 5" square stretched primed mini canvas
- ☐ Apple Barrel® Matte acrylic paint – Black
- ☐ DecoArt® Extreme Sheen™ - 24K Gold
- ☐ Apple Barrel® Multi Surface Satin acrylic paint - Candy Apple and Magenta
- ☐ Susan Bates® crochet hooks - 4mm, 5.5mm, and 8mm
- ☐ nail stylus dotting tool
- ☐ 1" wide flat paint brush
- ☐ Size 2 round paint brush
- ☐ ruler
- ☐ slate chalk marker
- ☐ damp rag and cotton swabs for cleanup
- ☐ kneaded eraser
- ☐ sealer of your choice

PREP

1. Paint the front and sides of the canvas with Black paint and allow to dry fully.

2. Practice writing the word "love" on some spare paper until you get it to your desired look. Write the word on the canvas using chalk or a pencil **(Fig. 1)**. If using a pencil, draw it on lightly so that you are not pushing too hard on the canvas.

3. With the ruler, draw a line above and below "love" so that you section off the canvas into 3 sections **(Fig. 2)**.

Fig. 1

Fig. 2

LET'S DOT!

Note: *Using a damp cloth, clean your tools after using each paint color.*

1. Using a size 2 round paint brush and 24K Gold metallic, paint the word, re-dipping the brush in paint as often as needed **(Fig. 3)**.

Fig. 3

2. Now to fill in the sections with DOTS! First, using a size 8mm crochet hook and Candy Apple paint, make random dots in the middle section around the word "love". These can be as random as you want to make them. Just be sure to leave some room for other size dots **(Fig. 4)**.

Fig. 4

3. Using the size 5.5mm crochet hook, make some more random dots in the middle section. But do leave room for some smaller dots **(Fig. 5)**.

Fig. 5

4. Using the size 4mm crochet hook, fill in some more of that section **(Fig. 6)**.

Fig. 6

5. Next, switch to the size 5 nail stylus and dot, dot, dot, to fill in the rest of the section that is bare **(Fig. 7)**.

Fig. 7

6. If you want, you can fill in more with tiny dots using the very smallest size 1 stylus, but it is perfectly okay to skip this step, too.

7. Alright, now for the top and bottom sections. Repeat Steps 2-6 using Magenta paint to fill the top and bottom sections **(Fig. 8)**.

Fig. 8

8. Allow paint to dry fully, at least a couple of hours.

9. Remove the guidelines with a kneaded eraser **(Fig. 9)**.

Fig. 9

10. Using the 4mm crochet hook, add a few small "top dots" to the largest dots using the opposite color for a nice little contrast and pop magic **(Fig. 10)**! Allow to dry again.

Fig. 10

11. Add a layer of sealer to the painting and you are ready to show this one off!

Way to go on another beautiful dot art painting!

Express your love for life with this sweet canvas.

Purple Passion Canvas

WHAT YOU'LL NEED

- ☐ 10" x 10" primed stretched canvas
- ☐ Apple Barrel® Matte acrylic paint - Black
- ☐ DecoArt® Americana® Neon Florescent acrylic paint - Ultraviolet
- ☐ DecoArt® Americana® Gloss Enamels™ multi-surface acrylic paint - Vivid Violet and White
- ☐ Apple Barrel® Multi Surface Satin acrylic - Princess Purple and Wisteria
- ☐ Martha Stewart Crafts® Pearl acrylic paints - Eclipse and Antique Silk
- ☐ wooden dowels – white (1/8"), pink (3/16"), lavender (1/4"), purple (5/16"), lime (7/16"), yellow (1/2"), and orange (5/8")
- ☐ nail stylus dotting tools
- ☐ kneaded eraser
- ☐ wide flat paint brush
- ☐ slate chalk marker
- ☐ yardstick
- ☐ guideline stencil (from www.dotartdepot.com) or 360° protractor
- ☐ damp rag and cotton swabs for cleanup
- ☐ sealer of your choice

PREP

1. Prepare the canvas by painting a basecoat of Black paint using a wide brush for fast and even application. Allow to dry completely.

2. Using the yardstick and chalk, mark an X on the canvas by lining up the ruler from corner to corner **(Fig. 1)**. Now you know where the center of the canvas is. Use a guideline stencil or a 360° protractor to draw on a total of 16 slices **(Figs. 2a-2b)**. You can absolutely freehand this as well.

Fig. 1

Fig. 2a

Fig. 2b

LET'S DOT!

Note: *Using a damp cloth, clean your tools after using each paint color.*

1. Start with the center dot. Use the orange dowel and Princess Purple paint to make the first dot right in the middle of the canvas **(Fig. 3)**.

Fig. 3

2. The first ring is going to be made with Princess Purple paint and the size 5 nail stylus. Make a dot on each of the

8 guidelines (**Fig. 4**). Then make one dot in between each of those to get a total of 16 dots around the center dot (**Fig. 5**).

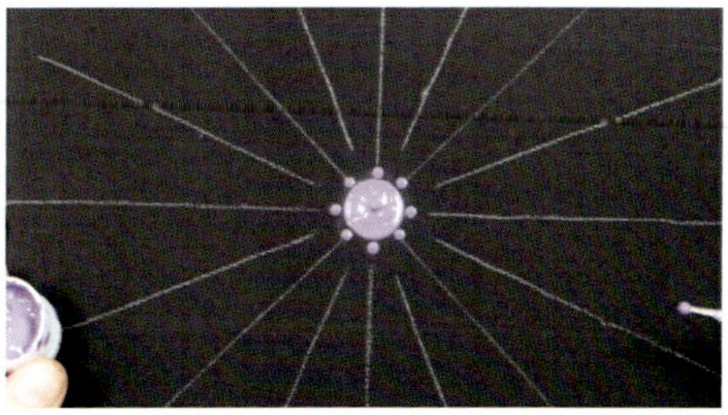

Fig. 4

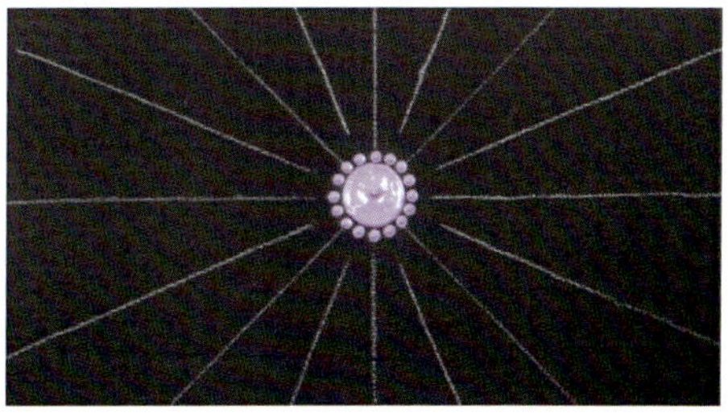

Fig. 5

3. The second ring will be made up of Wisteria paint, but this time using the white dowel. Place a dot right between, but on the outer edge of two dots from the previous ring, so that they are offset from each other (**Fig. 6**). Place a dot in the spaces between each of the previous 16 dots for a full second ring around the center dot (**Fig. 7**).

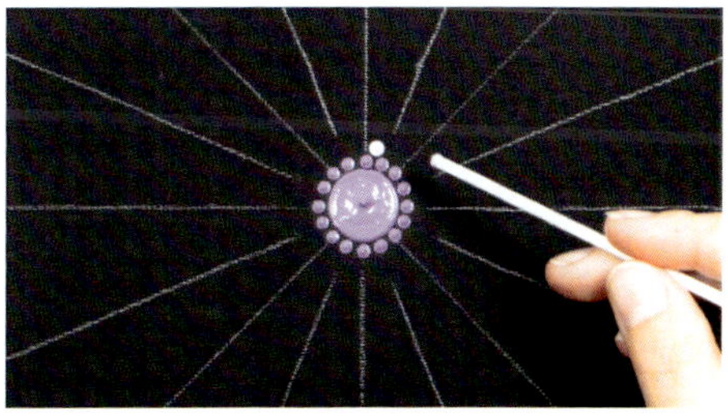

Fig. 6

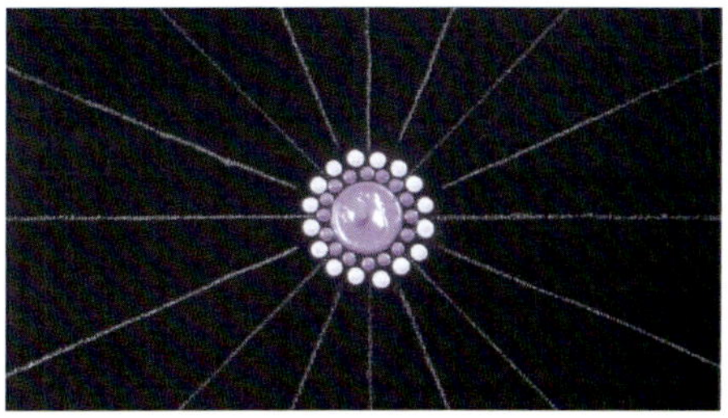

Fig. 7

4. Using the White paint and pink dowel, make a third ring of dots, offset from the last ring **(Fig. 8)**.

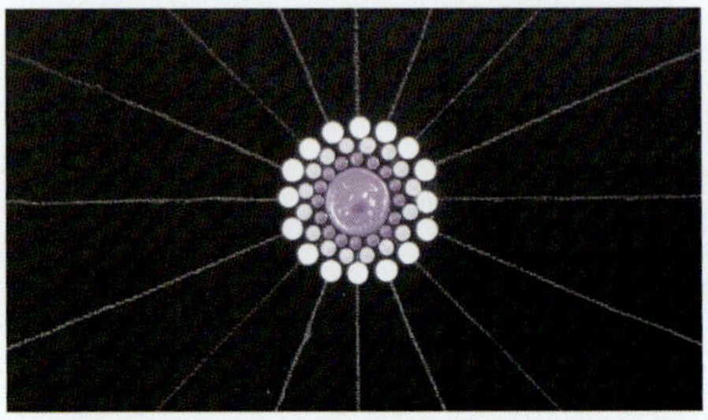

Fig. 8

5. And again, make one more ring, using the Eclipse paint and lavender dowel **(Fig. 9)**.

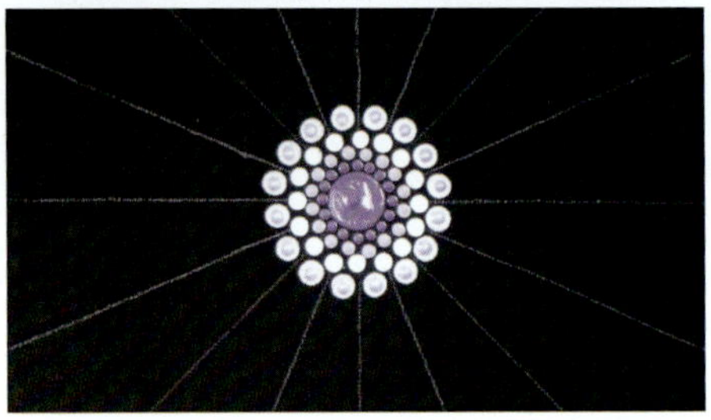

Fig. 9

6. Using the lime dowel and Ultraviolet paint, make a dot as if you were going to start another ring, but this time only place dots in between every other set of dots. You will have a total of 8 neon Ultraviolet dots **(Fig. 10)**.

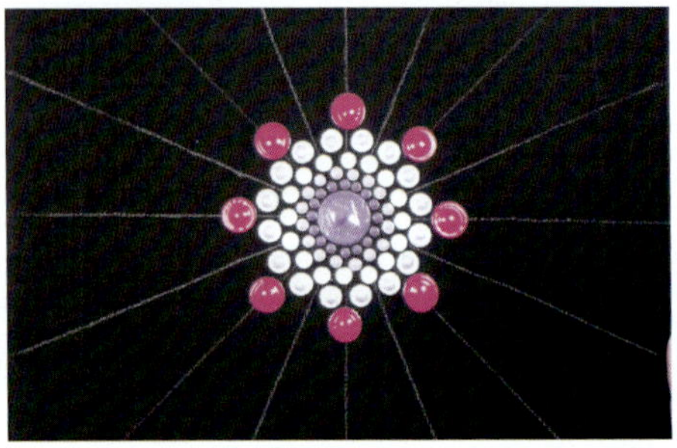

Fig. 10

7. Make the 8 neon dots into "petals" by wrapping little "bridges" of paint around each one. Using Ultraviolet paint and the white dowel, place your first dot lined up with the center of the outer edge of the large Ultraviolet dot. This I'll refer to as the main dot. Do this to each of the 8 dots **(Fig. 11)**.

Fig. 11

8. Using the size 5 nail stylus, make the first stylus dot right next to the main dot, close to the base or at the bottom of the main dot and dot all the way down to the base of the large dot, hugging to the curve **(Fig. 12)**. Re-dip the tool and do the same on the other side of the main dot **(Fig. 13)**. This is the first "bridge" of this petal. Repeat for all 8 dots **(Fig. 14)**.

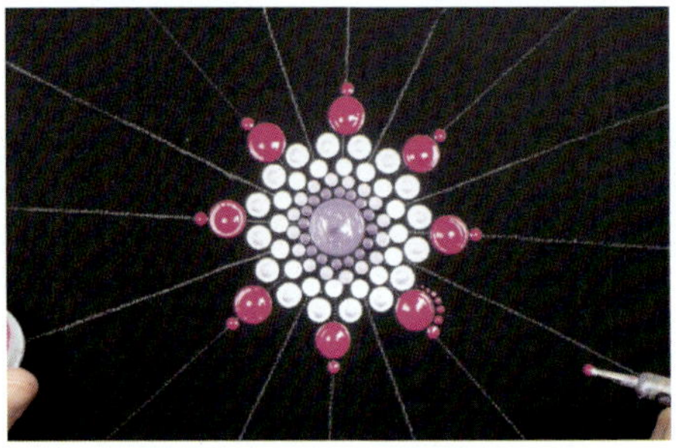

Fig. 12

Fig. 13

Fig. 14

9. For the next bridge, use the pink dowel and Vivid Violet paint to add a main dot above the last main dot **(Fig. 15)**. Following

Fig. 15

Fig. 16

Fig. 17

Fig. 18

up next to those with the white dowel **(Fig. 16)**. Then use the size 5 nail stylus to dot down to the base on each side **(Fig. 17)**. Again, repeat to make a bridge around each of the 8 petals **(Fig. 18)**.

10. For the final bridge on this petal, use the Antique Silk paint and the lavender dowel, and add the main dot, placing it right above the main dot of Vivid Violet **(Fig. 19)**. Repeat in the same manner as previous using the pink dowel, then the white dowel, and then dot all the way down with the size 5 stylus **(Fig. 20)**.

Fig. 19

Fig. 20

Fig. 21

11. Now make another layer of petals, offset from the first row of petals. This time, start off by placing the dots right in between the bridges, using the lime dowel for the center of each petal and using the Princess Purple paint **(Fig. 21)**.

12. Begin the first bridge using the same paint color and the pink dowel for the first main dot **(Fig. 22)**. Next to it dot all the way down with the size 5 stylus **(Fig. 23a-23b)**.

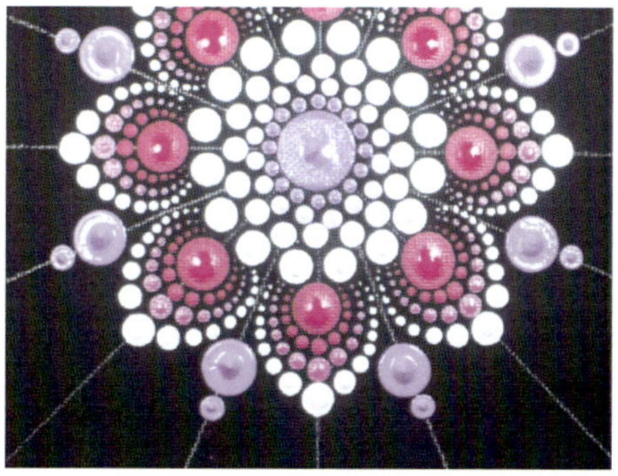

Fig. 22

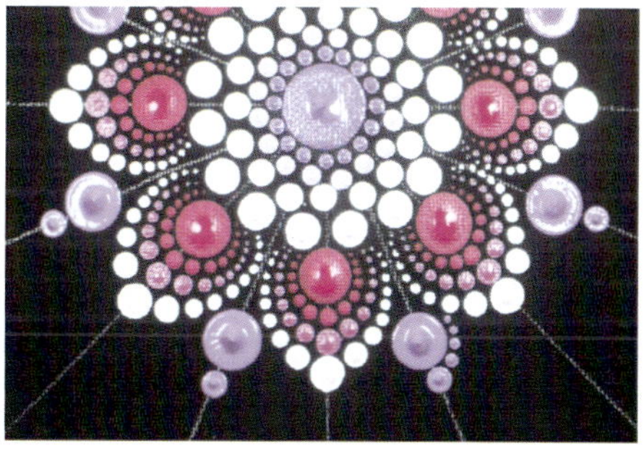

Fig. 23a

Fig. 23b

13. The next bridge will have a main dot made with Wisteria paint and the lavender dowel **(Fig. 24)**. Then add dots using the white dowel **(Fig. 25)**, Complete the bridge using the size 5 stylus **(Fig. 26)**.

Fig. 24

Fig. 25

Fig. 26

14. Next, use the purple dowel and the Eclipse paint for the main dot **(Fig. 27)**. Next to that add dots using the pink dowel **(Fig. 28)**, and then run the dots on down with the size 5 stylus **(Fig. 29)**. And this row of petals is complete!

Fig. 27

Fig. 28

Fig. 29

15. Make just one more row of petals, switching back to the violet set of paints, just like the first row of petals. Make these offset and in between the last row. Use the yellow dowel and Ultraviolet paint **(Fig. 30)**.

Fig. 30

16. Start the first main dot of this bridge with the pink dowel and Ultraviolet paint for the main dot **(Fig. 31)** and follow up with the size 5 stylus **(Fig. 32)** on either side of each of the 8 petals.

Fig. 31

Fig. 32

17. The next main dot will be made in the same manner as previous with the lavender dowel and Vivid Violet paint **(Fig. 33)**, followed by the white dowel **(Fig. 34)**, and then the size 5 stylus **(Fig. 35)**.

Fig. 33

Fig. 34

Fig. 35

18. The final bridge's main dot will be made in the same manner using the purple dowel and Antique Silk paint **(Fig. 36)** followed by the pink dowel **(Fig. 37)**, and then the size 5 stylus **(Fig. 38)**.

Fig. 36

Fig. 37

Fig. 38

19. Let the paint fully dry overnight or at least a couple of hours.

20. With the lavender dowel and White paint, make some "top dots" right on top, in the center of the large purple dots of the second row of petals **(Fig. 39a-39b)**.

Fig. 39a

Fig. 39b

21. Make a few tails of White dots heading outward on the sides of each of the outermost petals using the size 5 stylus **(Fig. 40)**.

Fig. 40

22. Again, allow the paint to fully dry before using the kneaded eraser to remove the guidelines **(Fig. 41)**.

Fig. 41

23. Add a coat of sealer to protect the paint.

Thank you for painting this with me! It's been fun!

Show your passion for purple with this fantastic explosion of color!

Sunflower Canvas

WHAT YOU'LL NEED

- ☐ 10" x 10" primed stretched canvas
- ☐ DecoArt® Americana® acrylic paint - Burnt Orange and Burgundy Wine
- ☐ DecoArt® Americana® Multi-Surface satin acrylic paint - Leprechaun
- ☐ DecoArt® Americana® Gloss Enamels™ multi-surface acrylic paint - Antique Gold
- ☐ Apple Barrel® Multi-Surface satin acrylic paint - Golden Yellow and Nectarine.
- ☐ Craft Smart® Multi-Surface Premium satin acrylic paint - Cocoa Bean
- ☐ wooden dowels - white (1/8"), lavender (1/4"), pink (3/16"), yellow (1/2"), and mint (7/8")
- ☐ nail stylus dotting tool
- ☐ kneaded eraser
- ☐ slate chalk marker
- ☐ compass
- ☐ yardstick
- ☐ wide, flat paint brush
- ☐ guideline stencil (from www.dotartdepot.com)
- ☐ damp rag and cotton swabs for cleanup
- ☐ sealer of your choice

PREP

1. Prepare the canvas by painting a basecoat of Burgundy Wine paint using the wide brush for fast and even application **(Fig. 1)**. Allow to dry completely.

Fig. 1

2. Using the yardstick and chalk or pencil, mark an X on the canvas by lining up the ruler from corner to corner **(Fig. 2)**. Now you know where the center of the canvas is.

3. Using the compass, set it to 2½" and draw a circle **(Fig. 3a-3b)**. This will be the center of the sunflower. Using the Burnt Orange paint and paint brush, paint the inside of that circle **(Fig. 4)**. Allow it to dry.

Fig. 2

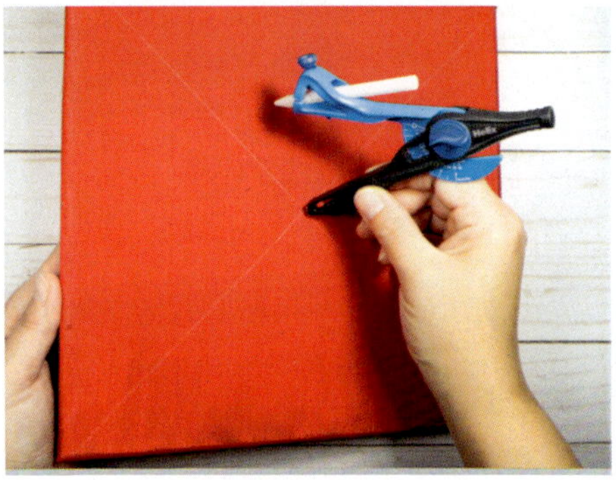

Fig. 3a

Fig. 3b

Fig. 4

LET'S DOT AND MIX PAINTS! (FUN STUFF!)

Note: *Using a damp cloth, clean your tools after using each paint color.*

1. Use the compass again and place it on the ½" mark and draw a guideline for the center dot (**Fig. 5**).

Fig. 5

2. I wanted an olive green for the center of the flower and didn't have the particular shade I was looking for, so I just made my own. Use the palette and pour a bit of Leprechaun into one well. Then, add to that only a drop or two of Cocoa Bean paint (**Fig. 6**) and mix. This will be the color you use for the center of the flower. Use the Mint dowel and dip it into the olive green paint and place the center dot in the middle of the canvas (**Fig. 7**). Let this dot dry completely before moving on.

Fig. 6

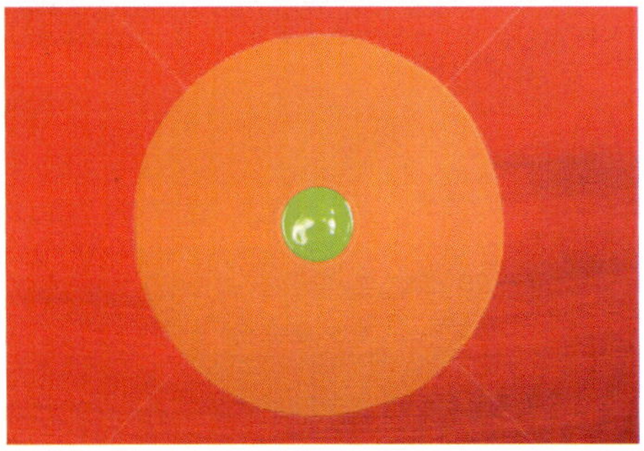

Fig. 7

3. Using either the guideline stencil or ruler and chalk or pencil, draw guidelines to divide the canvas into a total of 8 slices (**Fig. 8**).

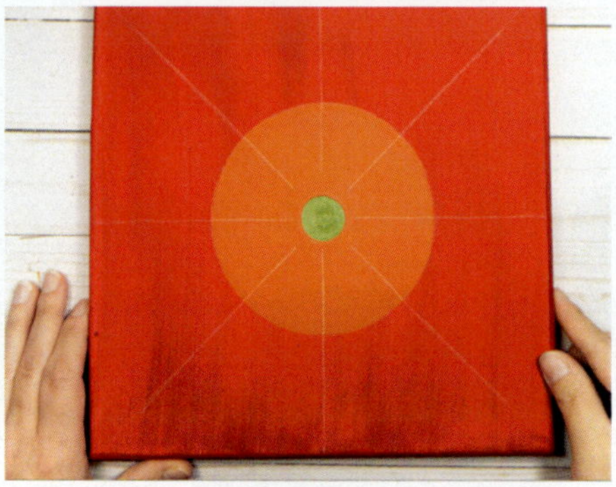

Fig. 8

4. With the size 3 nail stylus, make a crisscross of dots around the center dot, one to the top, bottom, left, & right. Then place a dot in between each of those dots to get 8 dots around the center (**Fig. 9**). And then place one more dot in between each of those dots to making 16 dots around the center dot (**Fig. 10**). And then place one more dot in between each of those dots to make a total of 32 dots around the center dot (**Fig. 11**).

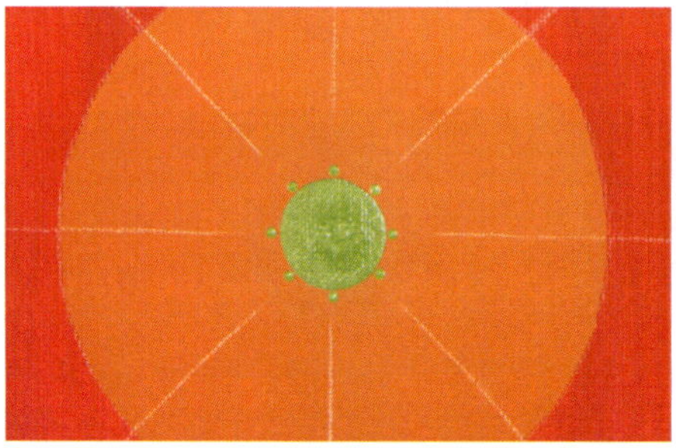

Fig. 9

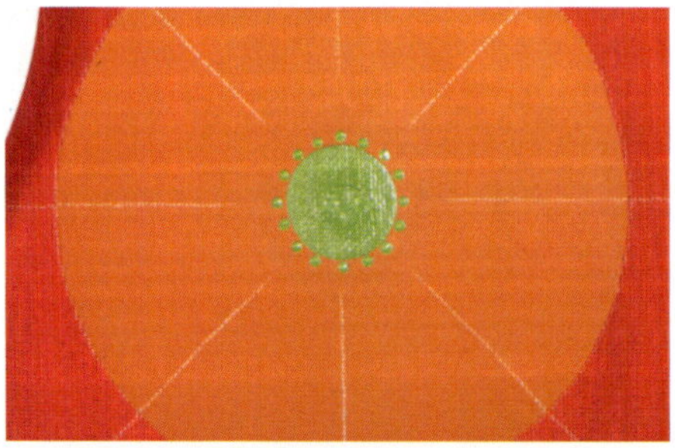

Fig. 10

Fig. 11

5. For the second ring, keep using the size 3 stylus and place a dot on the outer edge, in between two dots on the previous ring of dots. Make a dot in between each set of dots all the way around to make a full second ring of dots (**Fig. 12**). These dots are off set from the first ring of dots.

Fig. 12

6. Repeat Step 5, creating rings 3 and 4 using the size 5 stylus (**Fig. 13**). Each ring is off set from the previous ring.

Fig. 13

7. I wanted a lighter ring as I transitioned from green to brown so I added a little Antique Gold to the olive green mixture **(Fig. 14)**. Use this for the next ring using the white dowel **(Fig. 15)**.

Fig. 14

Fig. 15

8. Now, add Cocoa Bean paint into the lighter green color in a separate well **(Fig. 16)**. (Reserve some of the previous color in case you need a drop.) Use this paint and the white dowel to make the next ring **(Fig. 17)**.

Fig. 16

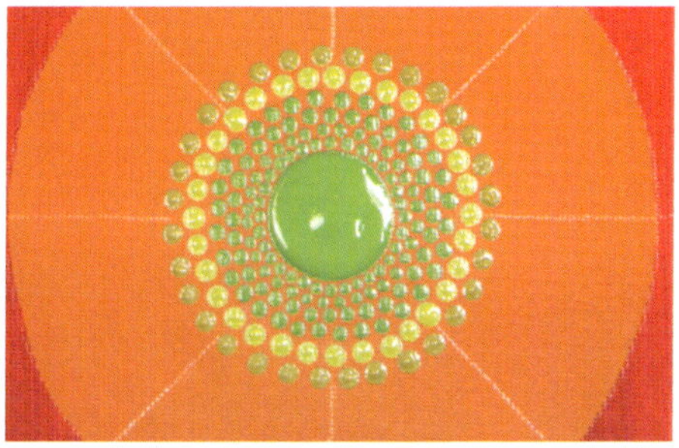

Fig. 17

9. Add a little bit more Coffee Bean paint and mix. Use this and the pink dowel for the next ring **(Fig. 18)**.

Fig. 18

10. Again, add a little bit more Cocoa Bean paint and mix. Use this and the pink dowel for the next ring **(Fig. 19)**.

Fig. 19

11. Using straight Coffee Bean paint and the lavender dowel, make the next two rings (**Fig. 20**). And the center of the flower is done! Now for the petals.

Fig. 20

12. Mix the Golden Yellow and Nectarine paints together at about a 1:1 ratio (**Fig. 21**). Use this and the yellow dowel to make the base dots for the petals, putting one dot on each of the 8 guidelines at the outer edge of the center of the flower (**Fig. 22**).

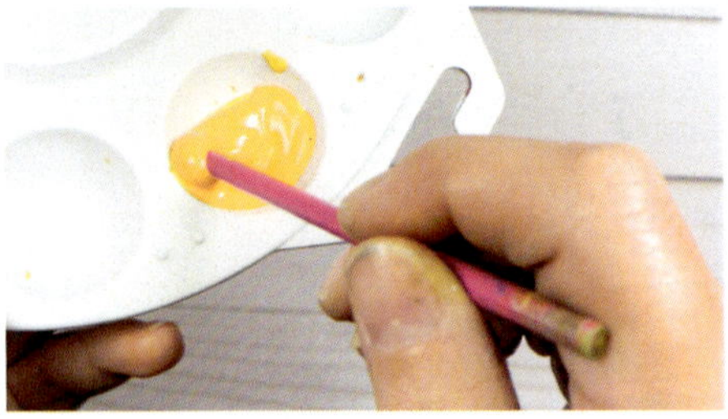

Fig. 21

Fig. 22

13. Now make the 8 dots into "petals" by wrapping little "bridges" of paint around each one. Using the size 5 nail stylus and Golden Yellow paint, start off with the first stylus dot lining up in the center of the outer edge of the large dot and dot all the way down to the base of the large dot, hugging to the curve (**Fig. 23**). Re-dip the tool in paint and re-dot the first initial dot and dot all the way down to the base of the other side (**Fig. 24**). This is the first "bridge" of this petal. Repeat to all 8 dots (**Fig. 25**).

Fig. 23

Fig. 24

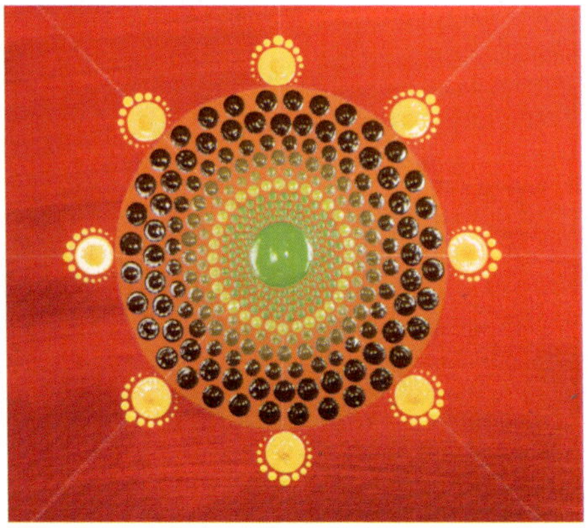

Fig. 25

14. For the main dot of the second bridge, use the pink dowel to make one dot right above the main dot of the previous bridge. Do this to all eight "petals". This will be the main dot on the second bridge and will start to make the eight petals larger (**Fig. 26**).

Fig. 26

15. Now, using the size 5 nail stylus, make the first stylus dot right next to the main dot, close to the base or at the bottom of the main dot and dot all the way down to the base, hugging the previous bridge of dots (**Fig. 27**). There is no particular number of dots to fit in there, just whatever works that you are comfortable with placing in that space. However, I find it helpful to count along. I was able to fit about 8 down each side so I counted, "one, two, three, four, five, six, seven, eight." Re-dip the stylus in paint and dot down

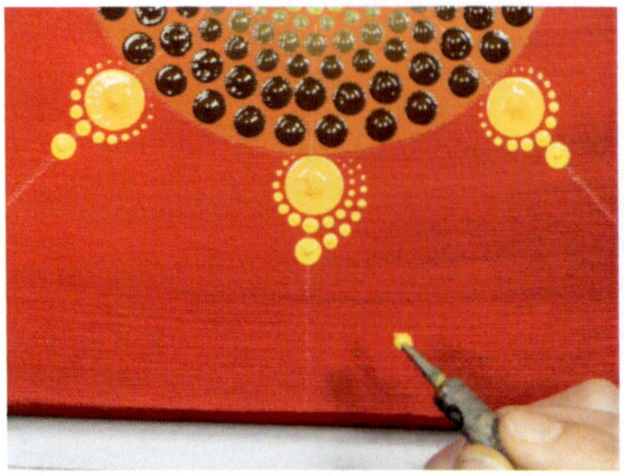

Fig. 27

the other side (**Fig. 28**). Now your petals are growing! Do this to each petal.

Fig. 28

16. For the next bridge's main dot, use the lavender dowel (**Fig. 29**). Follow with the size 5 stylus and only dot about halfway down the side of the previous bridge (**Fig. 30**). Repeat to all 8 petals.

Fig. 29

Fig. 30

Fig. 31

17. Repeat Step 16 for the next two bridges (**Fig. 31**).

18. Using the size 5 nail stylus, start in between each of the petals, about 1" up from the center and make a "tail" of dots toward the center (**Fig. 32**). Re-dip the tool and starting opposite the largest dot of the tail, dot in the outward direction as far as you want (**Fig. 33**). These do not have to be straight lines, and I made mine curve like a natural flower's petals would do.

Fig. 32

Fig. 33

19. Re-dip the tool and repeat Step 18 right next to the previous row (**Fig. 34**). Do this as many times as you want to add whatever thickness you desire to these petals (**Fig. 35**). I made mine random, making some of my petals 4 rows wide and some 5 rows (**Fig. 36**). Mix it up and have fun here.

Fig. 34

Fig. 35

Fig. 36

20. Once completely dry, use the kneaded eraser to remove the guidelines before adding a coat of sealer. (Once you seal them, you can't remove them.)

Enjoy your new sunflower painting!

Thank you so much for painting with me. Please join me on my YouTube channel for all kinds of other fun dot art designs!

Library of Congress Control Number: 2019952417.

Made in U.S.A.

Copyright © 2020 by Leisure Arts, Inc., 104 Champs Blvd., STE 100, Maumelle, AR 72113-6738, www.leisurearts.com. All rights reserved. This publication is protected under federal copyright laws. Reproduction or distribution of this publication or any other Leisure Arts publication, including publications which are out of print, is prohibited unless specifically authorized. This includes, but is not limited to, any form of reproduction or distribution on or through the Internet, including posting, scanning, or e-mail transmission.

We have made every effort to ensure that these instructions are accurate and complete. We cannot, however, be responsible for human error, typographical mistakes, or variations in individual work.

Production Team: Technical Editor – Lisa Lancaster; Graphic Designer – Lori S. Malkin; Photo Stylist – Lori Wenger; Photographer – Jason Masters.